MASTER YOUR ATTACHMENT STYLE

LEARN HOW TO BUILD HEALTHY & LONG-LASTING RELATIONSHIPS

SCOTT A. YOUNG

CONTENTS

INTRODUCTION

---

*The propensity to make strong emotional bonds to particular
individuals is a basic component of human nature.*

— *JOHN BOWLBY*

I first became aware of *attachment theory* a couple of years ago when
I stumbled upon some YouTube videos one lazy Saturday morning.
They explained why some people, especially those with past trauma,
have trouble with intimacy. As it turns out, even who we are as a
partner is influenced by the amount of love and attention we were
given as babies. The funny thing was, I used to think it was common
to make huge compromises in some relationships. I never questioned
why some of my partners asked for too much, and some asked for too

little. However, the deeper I looked into attachment theory, the more I began to understand how much influence my upbringing had.

I used to think each relationship I had was unique. After all, the reason for the breakup was never the same. But then, when I started learning more about attachment styles, I began to realize that there were recurring patterns I had not figured out before. I think the problem with not knowing anything about attachment theory is that you fail to see the signs even if they are right in front of you. We've all gone on dates. I'm pretty sure we've all had at least one person who refused to talk about their emotional side, even if you were already on the third date. They would often redirect the conversation so that you only conversed about general things, like hobbies, jobs, and favorite movies - topics that only touched the surface. Perhaps you went out with someone who overshared on the first date and incessantly tried to seek validation from you. In the eyes of someone aware of attachment theory, it's easy to tell what attachment style they have.

But, before we can fully grasp the complexities of adult attachment theory, we must take one step back and revisit our childhood. Sometime between the 1920s and 1930s, experts warned parents that showering their children with love and attention would result in emotionally stunted children. They suggested that parents shouldn't pick up their baby when they cried, or else they would become spoiled. In fact, in 1928, American psychologist John Broadus Watson wrote a best-selling book called *Psychological Care of Infant and Child*. In the book, he defined a happy child as one who only cries when hurt physically; is self-reliant, independent, and adaptable; learns to accept things without questioning them, and forms an emotional attachment to neither person nor object. It was not until the mid-1940s that scientists finally understood just how important the bond between mother and child is.

Attachment theory first got its name from British psychoanalyst John Bowlby. Bowlby believed that an infant develops a strong attachment towards the primary caregiver, who constantly provides comfort and security during signs of danger. He hypothesized that an infant's attachment to a primary caregiver was not based on who provided sustenance. Instead, he discovered that a child developed an attachment towards the one who could cater to their emotional needs. The caregiver would be the child's *secure base,* which led to what we now call the *dependency paradox.* If a child could rely on the caregiver to provide security and comfort, they became bolder and more independent.

Mary Ainsworth supported this belief by conducting her *Strange Situation Test.* In the 1970s, Ainsworth wanted to observe up close the attachment between mother and child. She did this through a series of eight stages that lasted three minutes each. First, the mother and her baby went inside a room with toys. Next, a stranger joined the two, and the mother left the room. Then, the mother returned, and the stranger exited the room. Next, the mother left the room, and the child was alone. Then, the stranger entered and was alone with the child. Lastly, the mother returned to the room, and the stranger left. Ainsworth was able to observe different reactions among the babies. From the sample population, she identified three attachment styles. She called *secure* babies those who felt distressed when the mother left but immediately felt reassured when she returned to the room.

The second one Ainsworth identified was the *insecure-ambivalent (anxious)* style. These babies felt distressed when the mother left. When she returned, the baby approached the mother but engaged in what we call protest behavior. The last one Ainsworth identified was the *insecure-avoidant* style. Babies that belonged to this category showed no signs of distress when the mother left the room and paid little interest to her when she returned. In 1990, psychologists Mary Main and Judith Solomon introduced a style that is considered rare among our population. It is the *disorganized (fearful-avoidant)* attachment style. Children with a disorganized attachment love their parents but, at the same time, fear them. They are constantly on edge and don't know what reaction to expect from their parents.

We all know that a child's environment shapes so much of their personality. If, as a baby, they learn that their needs aren't being met on purpose, they end up believing they need to "suck it up" because it doesn't matter. Therefore, they develop insecure attachment styles. Alternatively, attachment styles are something we subconsciously develop as we grow older because of the environment we grew up in. For example, if a child grew up in a loving home wherein their needs were always met, chances are, they become secure partners. However, if they grew up in an environment where their fight-or-flight mode was repeatedly activated, they subconsciously develop insecure attachment styles. If their single mom used to date sleazy men, the individual often grew up subconsciously dating the same kind of men.

And yet, despite everything we've come to know about attachment theory, it seems as if we've only touched the surface. Attachment styles should not be viewed in black and white. Your attachment styles are dependent on the different people in your life. For example, you may have a secure attachment towards your romantic partner but have an avoidant attachment towards a parental figure. Despite Bowlby believing our adult attachment styles are a product of our childhood, more research has come out over the years presenting other factors that may have affected the development of our attachment styles.

As we carry on with this book, we will answer some questions about attachment theory. Is a person's attachment style the sole determinant of how successful a potential relationship will be? Can a person's style change over time? Do previous dating experiences influence our attachment styles? While we will talk about Ainsworth's three attachment styles in-depth, we will also shed some light on the one attachment style not many people know or talk about—fearful-avoidant. Why wasn't this style identified until much later on?

In chapter 2, we will explore all possible factors that lead to these insecure attachment styles. We will talk about attachment as a biological and social necessity. There are two hormones that have a deep influence on our biological development. If a child were to be placed under stress for prolonged periods, how do you think these hormones would affect the child? There is also one other thing that is not often discussed in attachment theory, but we will discuss it in this book. That is how father-child attachments differ from mother-child relationships. Furthermore, we will explore Anthony Robbins' concept of the six human needs and how these needs are ranked based on your core wounds.

You will also learn how to identify attachment styles early in a relationship and how to deal with them. We will discuss each of the attachment style's defining traits and how they differ from each other. We will also explore whether sexual orientation has anything to do with a person's attachment style. Lastly, we will talk about one topic that not everyone seems to be familiar with: limerence. Just how different is it from love?

This book aims to help you understand how your past trauma affects how you view people, intimate relationships, and the world. This book is for you if you want nothing more than to build stronger and better relationships in your life. Perhaps you have noticed recurring patterns in your relationships but could not quite pinpoint what the commonality was. Maybe you have had trouble connecting with your partner on a deeper level, and you're not sure how to do it. Or perhaps you have a friend or a family member that you cannot seem to bond with. For whatever reason it may be, this book is for you, especially if you dream of creating deep and long-lasting relationships with the people in your life.

By the time you finish reading this book, you'll emerge with a clearer understanding of why you are now the way you are. You will also have the tools you need to navigate personal and romantic relationships to create healthy, lasting, and secure relationships.

1

UNDERSTANDING ATTACHMENT STYLE AND WHY IT'S SO IMPORTANT TO MASTER YOURS

THE BIRTH OF ATTACHMENT THEORY

*A**ttachment theory* is a psychological theory revolving around the idea that our romantic and platonic relationships with others result from how much affection we received during infancy. As children, we relied on our primary caregivers to provide a sense of security and comfort. However, some of us were not given the affection we sought as children. As a result, insecure attachment styles were born.

Attachment theory was formulated in the 1950s by psychoanalyst John Bowlby. However, before Bowlby formulated this theory, many psychologists had already studied attachment behaviors. Bowlby was fascinated with Konrad Lorenz's study of imprinting in goslings and Harry Harlow's study of attachment behavior in rhesus monkeys.

Deriving data from psychoanalyst James Robertson's work, Bowlby studied how the separation between mother and child affected their behavior. He identified three phases: Protest, Despair, and Detachment. *Protest* happens immediately after the child is separated from its maternal care. This phase lasts from a couple of hours up to a week or more. The child appears visibly distressed at the absence of their maternal figure and displays behavior (such as crying) to regain contact. The next phase, *despair*, shows the child gradually withdrawing. They may still cry and show signs of distress but are now more inactive and quiet. The last phase is *detachment*. Detachment was often viewed as a sign of recovery. The child no longer resists care from strangers and may even go back to being sociable. However, when the mother visits, the child may seem to address her as a mere stranger, seeming distant and apathetic.

Bowlby created his attachment theory to explain the relationship between a child's attachment behavior and their attachment to parental figures in their life. According to Bowlby, *attachment* is the unique relationship between a child and their caregiver that sets the foundation for healthy development. In other words, it is a child's bond to their primary caregiver. On the other hand, *attachment behavior* is any behavior a child exhibits to achieve or maintain proximity with a specific figure. Bowlby believed that attachment behavior is a behavioral system designed to increase an individual's chances of survival.

A child's first social attachment sets the tone for their personality. During the most crucial stage of a child's development, a child hungers for a mother figure's love and presence the way they crave food. If there is an absence of the care they seek, they will suffer in some aspects of their personality. In the next chapter, we will explore the difference between mother-child attachment and father-child attachment.

Behavior is known to be an environmentally stable character, given that the environment also remains stable. In the case of *nature* versus *nurture,* as long as children are raised in similar environments, their attachment behaviors are simply dependent on genetic differences. However, because no environment is the same and people constantly need to adapt, there will always be a difference in our coping mechanisms. If the environment then varies from one child to another, the differences in attachment behaviors become more pronounced. Even in twin siblings, it was proven that attachment patterns rarely rely on genetics and are more influenced by environmental factors.

An adult's attachment behavior is simply a persistence of their childhood attachment behavior. In moments of despair or calamity, an adult's initial reaction is to seek the comfort of a trusted individual, just like how a child would seek the caregiver's comfort during moments of sickness. This is an entirely natural response.

Most of the early research conducted by psychologists about attachment was done on animals. However, there is no mistaking that humans and animals share one thing in common—our chances of survival increase when we form attachments.

BEHAVIORAL SYSTEM

The concept of a behavioral system is probably Bowlby's most significant contribution to psychology. A *behavioral system* is a product of evolution whose primary function is to ensure survival and reproduction. He suggested that children are far from being a blank slate when born and have an innate behavioral system waiting to be activated.

A behavioral system is believed to be developed from specific neural programs that control behavioral sequences' activation and deactivation. These behavioral sequences are postulated to be responsible for searching and forming an attachment bond and providing care.

Although behavioral systems share the common goal of increasing chances of survival, an attachment behavioral system's primary biological function is to promote a closeness to an attachment figure. When an individual is presented with triggers, the behavioral attachment system is activated. Triggers can be external cues, such as a stranger's presence, or internal cues, like emotions and worries. When the system is activated, the individual engages in a primary strategy to accomplish its main function. In the behavioral attachment system, the primary strategy is engaging in specific behaviors, such as crying or reaching out to the attachment figure. Suppose the primary strategy is unable to accomplish the goal. In that case, a secondary strategy may be used, such as hyper-activating the system or detaching from it.

Humans are complex beings and therefore need the help of more than one behavioral system to function. More often than not, the behavioral attachment system works together with other systems in our body. In relationships, attachment behaviors usually go hand-in-hand with caregiving and sexual behaviors.

MARY AINSWORTH AND HER CONTRIBUTION

Another key person who aided in attachment theory development was psychologist Mary Ainsworth. It's hard to talk about Bowlby without mentioning the work of Ainsworth.

Ainsworth's contribution to attachment theory began with her study in Africa. Before her two-year stay in Uganda, she collaborated with John Bowlby and James Paterson in London for four years. In 1954, Ainsworth flew to Uganda to stay at the East African Institute for Social Research, where she observed infant attachment behavior in the villages surrounding Kampala. She wanted to observe the Ugandan tradition of separating an infant from their mother for a few days during the weaning stage so that infants will "forget the breast." However, she discovered that many Ugandans had already stopped practicing the tradition. Instead, she studied the differences in infant-mother interactions among 26 families for nine months.

It was in her Ugandan study that she introduced the term *maternal sensitivity*. Ainsworth defined maternal sensitivity as accurately interpreting and providing an appropriate response to a child's discreet or apparent signals. The most central idea of maternal sensitivity revolved around whether the mother would act on these signals or not. However, it wasn't until she conducted her Baltimore study that she could fully expand on maternal sensitivity. The Baltimore study served the same purpose as the Ugandan study—to observe infant-mother interactions, but this time in richer detail. Participants of her research were 26 white middle-class mothers. The group was separated into two. The first group consisted of 15 families that would receive four-hour home visits, starting after the 3rd week of the child's birth, at three-week intervals until the 54th month. The second group consisted of 11 families who had weekly two-hour visits, starting after the 6th week.

The results of her Baltimore study showed the four elements needed to determine the sensitivity to an infant's signals: 1) awareness, 2) accurate interpretation, 3) appropriate responsiveness, and 4) prompt responsiveness. It was and still is, argued that maternal sensitivity was the forerunner of attachment theory. Towards the end of her Baltimore study, Ainsworth conducted one of the most recognized tests in the world of psychology. It was called the *Strange Situation Test*. This was done to understand different attachment styles towards mothers with one-year-old babies. These infants were the same participants from the Baltimore study.

In summary, the *Strange Situation Test* was done by placing a one-year-old in a room filled with toys. First, the mother was present in the room, then absent, and then she returned. This was an opportunity for Ainsworth to observe how children used their primary caregivers as a secure base during curious exploration.

Ainsworth identified three main attachment patterns from the study: B, A, and C. Pattern B infants were called *secure* babies. Pattern A infants were called *anxious-avoidant,* and Pattern C infants were called *anxious-resistant* babies.

Ainsworth's contribution to attachment theory is vital for three reasons. First, it provided reliable evidence of how attachments worked in safe and threatening situations. Second, she was the first to classify the differences in attachment behaviors. Third, she was one of the first people to support the theory that infant attachment behaviors directly correlated with how caregivers responded to them during the first year of life. Her study paved the way for more psychologists to explore the implications of adult attachments.

STAGES OF ATTACHMENT IN CHILDREN

While Ainsworth (1967) conducted a study observing attachment behavior between mothers and their children, Rudolph Schaffer and Peggy Emerson (1964) also tried to figure out how attachment in children worked. Their study found that children underwent different attachment stages in their first year of life.

The first stage happens from birth to six weeks. In this stage, the infant is asocial and is not ready to form any attachment towards a designated primary caregiver.

After six weeks until the 7th month, the baby starts recognizing sounds, sights, and feelings. Furthermore, they also begin to form an attachment with the most familiar caregiver and start distinguishing familiar and unfamiliar faces.

The third stage occurs from the baby's 7th to 9th months. They start showing a strong preference for the appointed primary caregiver. Aside from that, they also begin showing signs of fear when introduced to strangers. They may also show signs of distress when separated from their caregiver.

The fourth and final stage happens during the 11th month and onwards. In this stage, the child begins developing strong emotional bonds with more than one caregiver. These people could be grandparents, siblings, or another parent. However, the child creates a hierarchy in terms of preference. They may form a strong bond with three people but will still prefer one over the other, regardless of the situation.

ATTACHMENT AND CULTURE

Bowlby hypothesized that attachment theory was a product of human evolution, and therefore, it was universal. Ainsworth's findings from both the Ugandan and Baltimore studies led her to conclude that maternal sensitivity was a universal construct. Her results also backed Bowlby's claim that attachment patterns were similar, regardless of culture.

In numerous cross-cultural studies, three similarities always popped up:

1. A secure attachment was the most common style and was believed to be the most desirable.

2. Maternal responsiveness influenced the infant's attachment behavior.

3. Children with a secure attachment were often predicted to be more friendly and cognitive.

However, in a constantly evolving society, more and more differences begin to pop up, such as religion, social status, ethnicity, and education. John Bowlby and Mary Ainsworth may have set the wheels in motion to develop attachment theory, but we have come a long way since then.

THE DEPENDENCY PARADOX AND A SECURE BASE

In some Western cultures, depending on an individual is considered a sign of weakness. Yet, Bowlby's attachment theory disputes this. Bowlby theorized that an individual must have a secure base to achieve their true potential. This was Bowlby's entire premise about attachment theory. A *secure base* is support that partners provide to help the individual be more confident and daring in exploring the world.

Bowlby believed that when parents laid out a secure base, a child became increasingly confident in exploring an environment. This is because the child knows that their parents are available and ready to cater to them should they be needed. A secure base goes hand-in-hand with the haven of safety. A secure base is the confidence a child has to explore their environment. Meanwhile, the *haven of safety* is the confidence that the child has, knowing they can go back during stressful situations.

Suppose parents prove that they are sensitive and responsive to a child's needs time and time again. In that case, the child will begin to associate the parent with a secure base. Bowlby emphasized that a child may only start to grasp the concept of a secure base when they start recognizing a parent's responsiveness in times of distress. For an infant, distress may either indicate a potential internal/external threat or concern about the presence and availability of their chosen attachment figure.

Dependence on a partner is an instinct. If a partner is sensitive about providing the support and comfort an individual needs, they actually encourage independence and self-reliance instead of impeding it. This is known as the *dependency paradox*. It may seem like a weird idea. How can dependence on our partner teach us how to become independent people? Well, that's why it's a paradox. Think of it like this: If you want to achieve happiness in life, find an individual whom you can rely on to share the journey with through your highs and lows. Once you begin to understand how having a reliable partner affects your overall happiness, you begin to grasp the concept of attachment theory.

To further explain the concept of the dependency paradox and a secure base, we go back to where it all started—our childhood. While studies suggest that attachment patterns have different characteristics in children and adults, it is worth noting how a parents' responsiveness, or lack thereof, manifests itself in the child's behavior. Unfortunately, most of the studies conducted were only focused on the mother as the caregiver. There are little to no studies involving fathers as the primary attachment figure. However, it would be interesting to see how a father's parenting influences a child's attachment behavior.

ATTACHMENT PATTERNS IN CHILDREN

During Ainsworth's *Strange Situation Test,* she only identified three attachment patterns. However, she had difficulty categorizing the infants into the three classifications because some of their behavior did not fit into what they were classified as. For example, children labeled secure tended to exhibit dismissive behavior in certain situations. A few years later, Mary Main and Judith Solomon (1986) introduced a fourth style, *disorganized.* In the test, infants were classified based on their reactions during their maternal figures' absence and presence. If an infant failed to display consistent behavior throughout the test, they were classified as disorganized.

Ainsworth believed that two conditions contributed to the development of a child's attachment pattern during the first year of life. One, a mother's sensitivity in responding to the child's needs. Two, the frequency and nature of contact between the primary caregiver and the child.

Parents of *securely attached* children are emotionally consistent and respond quickly to their children's needs. These children have supportive parents who taught them that vulnerability is not bad and that their needs matter. As a result, the child is secure and autonomous.

When a parent is often absent from a child's life, be it physically, emotionally, or intellectually, the child eventually learns how to self-soothe. Since children are naturally programmed to rely on their caregivers for survival, absent parents result in *dismissive-avoidant* children. This child starts believing their needs do not matter and starts feeling detached from their primary caregivers.

A child becomes *anxiously attached* when the caregiver is often absent and inconsistent in providing support. Inconsistent parenting may be manifested as a parent who consistently offers support but cannot be physically present all the time. Anxiously attached children are hypervigilant and in constant fear of abandonment from their caregivers.

On the other hand, *fearful-avoidant* children could, unfortunately, be victims of abuse at home. Aside from the abuse, it could be paired with inconsistent parenting from one or both parents. Children possessing a fearful-avoidant attachment may have self-esteem and trust issues. Furthermore, they distrust adults and are prone to developing behavioral problems.

ATTACHMENT PATTERNS IN ADULTS

This chapter will briefly discuss attachment patterns in adults so you gain a basic understanding of the different attachment styles, and we will further explore this topic in the third chapter.

Securely attached people are those who are low on avoidance and low on anxiety. They are not afraid of conflict resolution and are comfortable with intimacy without feeling overwhelmed.

On the other hand, *anxious-preoccupied* people are low on avoidance but high on anxiety. They crave intimacy and approval but are insecure about their relationships. They are usually mistrustful of their partners and typically have negative feelings towards the relationship during minor signs of conflict.

Dismissive-avoidant people are high on avoidance but low on anxiety. They don't mind intimacy, but they immediately withdraw and keep their distance as soon as they get overwhelmed. Their independence and freedom are high up on the list of priorities.

Fearful-avoidant people are high on both avoidance and anxiety. They have mixed feelings about a relationship. They crave closeness and intimacy, yet they also value their independence and freedom.

Wondering what your attachment style is?
Download my attachment style "cheat sheet" by going to
MasterYourAttachmentStyle.com/CheatSheet

UNDERSTANDING HOW YOUR ATTACHMENT PATTERN IS INFLUENCED

As previously stated, much of who we are now is a product of our childhood experiences. The first few years are the most crucial and set the tone for who we will be when we become adults. The most significant factor influencing the formation of our attachment pattern is our parents' ability to show up. If a child's parents were emotionally available, consistent, and predictable, they would most likely develop a secure attachment. However, if the child had parents who constantly invalidated the child's feelings, were emotionally volatile, and absent, they grew up with either of the three insecure attachment patterns.

Furthermore, a child's attachment pattern is not only influenced by how responsive both parents were. It may also be affected by the environment that they were raised in. Attachment also plays a significant role in regulating our stress response. When a human is born, the presence of a fully developed stress response system, the *HPA axis*, is already at work. Oliveira (2019) discovered that children who exhibited an insecure attachment had increased cortisol levels after being exposed to an initial stimulus. *Cortisol* is a hormone that is released during stressful situations. When immersed in a stressful situation, it temporarily turns off some of the body's systems that aren't needed. In other words, their brain uses an attachment to regulate their cortisol levels. Some studies have shown that insecurely attached children have higher cortisol levels than securely attached children during threatening situations. However, it was unclear which insecure attachment pattern was most affected.

Even if a child has supportive parents, they may still grow up manifesting an insecure attachment style if poor quality of caregiving is provided. If they grow up in a household where violence is often displayed, albeit not directed at them, there are still negative repercussions. Thus, when a child is exposed to a harsh environment, the quality of caregiving plays a very important role in the development of their attachments. Conversely, since all children are genetically different, caregiving behavior may only offer little influence on their attachment compared to other environmental factors.

One of the most profound things about attachment theory is discovering how it affects other aspects of our lives. So far, we have mostly talked about attachments in intimate relationships. What people fail to realize is that our attachment style expands past our romantic relationships. It may also affect our friendships and work relationships. People may have different attachments with the different people in their lives. A person may have a secure attachment towards their best friend but may have a fearful-avoidant attachment to a parental figure.

Let's take, for example, Jonathan. Due to his parents' inconsistency and living in a largely volatile household, he developed a disorganized attachment style. One day at work, a colleague comments about the project that Jonathan is working on, and Jonathan takes it personally. Many fearful-avoidants have self-worth issues. When Jonathan's colleague commented about his work, Jonathan took it personally because it triggered his self-esteem issues. However, Jonathan was not consciously aware of why he felt triggered. In his mind, he viewed his coworker as rude and nosy. Had he stopped to think about why he felt so strongly about it, he might have realized it was more about his unhealed wounds and less about his coworker.

Our attachment style influences even our most basic interactions with people. For example, an *anxious* person may be a people-pleaser simply because they crave validation from others. They fear that if they say no, they will not receive the love and affection they seek. On the contrary, our relationships may influence our attachment style, too. Let's look at a side-by-side comparison between a secure-anxious relationship and a dismissive-anxious relationship. When an anxious person is with a secure partner, they are less likely to engage in *protest behavior* because their partner does an excellent job providing the reassurance and intimacy that an anxious person needs. Protest behavior is an action that an individual engages in to re-establish a connection with another individual. Examples of protest behavior include: excessive calling/messaging, ignoring your partner, keeping score, acting hostile, and engaging in activities that purposely make your partner jealous. On the other hand, when a dismissive person and an anxious person are together, the anxious person would seem to be constantly in fight-or-flight mode. Due to the dismissive-avoidant person's natural tendency to sometimes shut off their feelings, the anxious person worries a lot and tries their best to reestablish a connection with their partner for fear of a breakup.

A dismissive-anxious relationship would seem like a dance between two birds. We don't exactly understand why, but dismissive people naturally gravitate toward anxious people and vice versa. Anxious people crave intimacy, connection, and validation, so they often pick a distant and often difficult partner to connect with. On the other hand, the dismissive-avoidant partner enjoys independence and tends to be distant. In turn, they choose a possessive partner who is constantly demanding attention.

WHY KNOWING YOUR ATTACHMENT STYLE MATTERS

After some of the things we've briefly discussed, you may wonder why it's so important to know about your attachment style. The more aware you are about your attachment style, the easier it will be to navigate life and work out your relationships with the people in your life. In an ideal world, all of our parents consistently showed up, and we are all securely attached. Sadly, this is not a perfect world, and we have no say in how our attachment styles were developed. The best thing to do is recognize your attachment style and understand why we react and feel the way we do in certain situations. Understanding attachment theory might help you better understand why you think the way you do and why you choose the people you choose. Furthermore, it will equip you with the necessary tools to make better and more informed decisions. When you finally understand the intricacies of attachment theory, you stop letting your unhealed childhood wounds dictate how you'll move forward with your life.

Look, there is simply nothing wrong with creating an attachment with others. We are human, and it is in our nature to form bonds with people in our life. If understood correctly, you can even turn the tables around and use your knowledge of attachment theory to your benefit. Once you figure out what kind of attachment you have, you can even slowly work on it to move towards becoming a more secure individual. Self-awareness plays a vital role in understanding exactly why we react the way we do.

Attachment styles also play an essential role for same-sex couples. For example, we have Jayden, a dismissive-avoidant. Jayden has been with his boyfriend, Tommy, for about a year when they finally talk about moving in together. When Tommy moved into Jayden's place, Jayden felt suffocated and started resenting Tommy and his presence. He wanted his freedom and independence back, and with Tommy constantly in his space, he felt as if he was losing it altogether. Fortunately for Jayden, he had been going to therapy to deal with his childhood trauma and, it was in one of his sessions, he found out about his attachment style. Thinking back to that session, Jayden understood that his lashing out was not because of Tommy. His reaction was because he had never tried stating the needs he wanted to be met. As a result, he sat down with Tommy and tried to ask for space while still showing that he cared for him and wanted to show up. Thankfully, Tommy understood that Jayden was not used to being in a situation like this and sometimes needed time to recharge to be emotionally available to his boyfriend once more.

Another reason you should understand attachment theory is to learn how to spot common behaviors and signs in other people. Awareness of the mechanisms of attachment theory will help you become a more understanding individual. When you begin to understand your attachment style and why you react a certain way, your interactions with other people will be a lot easier. While the end goal is to become a secure partner, change is not linear and certainly does not happen within a day. There will be times where you will slip up and go back to your old habits, but it's okay. Nobody will judge you for it. What matters is that you wake up every morning trying to be a better partner, friend, and coworker. The first and most crucial step to obtaining a secure attachment is acknowledging your past for what it is—trauma.

Now that you know the basics and the history of the development of attachment theory, we can begin to explore the birth of our attachment styles. In doing so, we also develop a better understanding of how our attachment patterns may interfere with some of our basic human needs.

2

THE BIRTH OF OUR ATTACHMENTS - EMBRACING OUR TRAUMAS

As stated in the first chapter, our attachment styles were developed based on the relationship we had with our parents when we were younger. That relationship became the blueprint for who we are today as a partner, friend, or coworker. As we enter adulthood, our encounters with different types of people also have a certain amount of influence on our attachment style. Therefore, as adults, our attachment style is a product of our childhood experiences and other adult relationships. So, while a person may have had a secure childhood, bad experiences in relationships may cause them to become insecure.

To illustrate this concept, imagine a girl named Gemma. Gemma grew up in a loving home where all her needs were met, and her parents were nothing less than supportive. As she became an adult and started dating people, she, unfortunately, had a lot of bad experiences. Once, she dated a girl who felt overly insecure to the point where she would get jealous if Gemma talked to other people. She also dated a guy who had commitment issues and ultimately cheated on her. Over time, Gemma's bad experiences led her to view relationships in a different light, and eventually, her once secure attachment had shifted into a dismissive-avoidant attachment.

ATTACHMENT AS A BIOLOGICAL NECESSITY

Some species of animals are born completely capable and self-sufficient. For humans, it's the opposite. When babies are born, it takes them about a year before they can walk without any assistance, yet that is only the beginning. Humans depend on a caregiver for nearly two decades before they're capable of exploring the world on their own. There is nothing wrong with it, as all of this time is necessary to develop the human brain for a functioning, logical individual.

What's impressive is that all of this is simply by design. After numerous studies observed caregiving in animals, it is safe to assume that attachments are necessary for survival and evolution. Some animals are born self-sufficient because they have to be constantly on the move, lest they become prey. On the other hand, children form an attachment with a primary caregiver to ensure their safety and development. This is because the first few years are the most important for cognitive development. Even into early adulthood, our brain's prefrontal cortex is still developing.

During our youth, a bond was necessary for survival and evolution. If you belonged to a group, your chances of survival significantly increased because more people could protect you from predators. Therefore, Bowlby believed our attachment existed for the sole reason of survival. However, Dr. Lois Murphy (1964) argued that an attachment behavior's primary function is so the infant can learn activities from the attachment figure that will guarantee survival. Bowlby countered Murphy's argument by saying that if the attachment behavior simply existed so an infant can learn activities vital to survival, why do people continue to have attachment behaviors well into adulthood, even though learning was long finished? Additionally, if that was the primary purpose of attachment, why would an attachment behavior be activated during minor signs of threat?

ATTACHMENT AS A SOCIAL NECESSITY

Human beings are social creatures. This is pretty much proven by the saying, "No man is an island," and it is true. No one can survive independently without support or connection from friends or family. In children, emotional neglect has an even more tangible result.

Several studies have been made about children who become "feral" due to limited human contact and emotional neglect. Although babies are born with a natural instinct to form a bond with a caregiver, this can be distorted when the caregiver shows inconsistency and emotional negligence. According to Teicher (2000), children who come from an emotionally neglectful household during their younger years exhibit some mental impairments. Neglected children have reduced growth in the left hemisphere and are at higher risk of depression. They also show increased sensitivity in their limbic system, making them at risk of developing anxiety disorders. Lastly, children who are not given adequate amounts of love and attention have reduced growth in the hippocampus. The hippocampus is a part of the limbic system responsible for memory and learning. If a hippocampus has reduced growth, the child may develop learning and memory disabilities. Therefore, parents must support their children in their early years. Children don't need expensive toys or destination holidays; they want their parents' time and attention.

Numerous studies have also been done on U.S. teenagers and college students. Subjects of these studies came from different ethnic backgrounds, yet there was a commonality among the subjects: attachment patterns affected a person's social skills. Secure students had minimal trouble adjusting, while insecure students were often faced with adjustment difficulties and self-esteem issues. Cooper et al. (1998) also discovered that anxious-avoidant females were more likely to have depression and anxiety versus females with other attachments.

Furthermore, a person's attachment behavior may also affect their friendships. In a study on American college students, Grabill and Kerns (2000) found that secure young adults were more involved in friendships than insecurely attached young adults. Securely attached young adults were more likely to open up and feel validated and understood by their peers. In another separate study, Parade, Leerkes, and Blankson (2010) also found that secure college students, both white and people of color, had improved friendships by the end of their first semester as a freshman.

With a significant amount of research to back this claim up, it is evident that attachment is both a biological and social necessity.

Without attachment, people simply cannot form genuine connections with others, and without this bond, the survival rate is significantly lower.

PARENTAL AFFECTION AND A CHILD'S NEEDS

Parents lead hectic lives, from working to raising their children. Although parents need to work hard to provide for their children, what children really need is their time and affection. Over the past ten years, studies have proven that parental affection influences the child's health and happiness later on in life.

When parents are warm and affectionate towards their children, it will result in a lifetime of positive results. Children who were provided with enough parental affection were reported to have higher self-esteem, improved academic performance, and fewer behavioral and psychological problems. On the contrary, neglected children were said to be aggressive, antisocial, and have lower self-esteem.

Even in adoption cases, the results were the same. Pace and Zavattin (2010) defined late-placed children as children adopted after the first year of life who had experienced a traumatic event from one parental figure. They observed that late-placed children had higher attachment insecurities than children raised by natural birth parents. However, a year after the adoption, these children positively changed their attachment styles. They also observed that it is possible for adopted children to develop a secure attachment towards their adoptive parents, given that secure parents also raise them. A separate study conducted on identical twins showed that whether they were biological or adoptive children, the mother's attachment was the key determinant of their attachment style, not their genetics. In conclusion, parents are responsible for creating positive interactions and enforcing positive behavior with their adopted children.

Earlier, we talked about the relationship between *cortisol* and attachment. Now, we will talk about another hormone that plays a role in our attachments—oxytocin. *Oxytocin* is a hormone responsible for female reproduction and certain aspects of human behavior, such as mother-infant attachment and pair bonding. It is sometimes referred to as the "cuddle hormone" because it is released whenever physical contact is received, such as hugging, holding hands, or cuddling.

Oxytocin has been discovered to be linked to a person's early caregiving experiences. For example, women with a history of child abuse were found to have lower oxytocin concentrations. The same results were found for men who had gone through an early parental separation. Although it offers no causation, it can be assumed that childhood trauma may impede the oxytocinergic system's development.

FATHER-CHILD ATTACHMENTS

The main reason why Bowlby created attachment theory was so he could dispute the argument that children form an attachment to their mothers because the mother provides oral gratification (i.e., breastfeeding). Therefore, there aren't many studies that focus on fathers as the primary attachment figures.

In Mary Ainsworth's Uganda study, she had noted that children could establish several attachments, including one with their father. Bretherton (2010) found that children have different relationships with their parents. For example, children viewed the mother as the caregiver, while the father was considered a playmate. Fathers usually take on the role of encouraging their children to partake in challenges and teaching them independence.

In a two-parent household, each parent fulfills a different role necessary to develop a secure base. One parent, usually the mother, is responsible for being a refuge in times of distress. In contrast, the other parent, usually the father, is responsible for providing a safe space for exploration and taking on new challenges. Regardless, both of these roles were seen as equally important in the child's psychological development. For a child to develop a secure attachment, they must have someone who offers comfort and pushes them to explore the world.

Kamza (2019) found that fathers tended to be fussier towards their sons and mothers towards their daughters. Fathers were found to interact less with their daughters than with their sons. The reason behind this hasn't been fully explored yet; however, assumptions can be made. When daughters reach adolescence, parents bear the task of preparing their children for the stereotypical gender role. For example, mothers may interact more with their daughters to teach them how to cook or dress, while fathers would prepare the son for roles he is expected to fulfill as a man.

A study by Brown et al. (2015) noted that a father's involvement and paternal sensitivity impacted a child's attachment. Fathers who were relatively insensitive but were highly involved led to securely attached children. On the other hand, children whose fathers were sensitive but relatively uninvolved were more likely to develop an insecure attachment pattern.

In another study, the impact of a bad father-daughter relationship during adolescence was also observed. Jain (2015) concluded that daughters with a secure attachment towards their fathers had higher self-esteem and social competence. They also displayed exceptional communication satisfaction and communication adaptability. On the contrary, a poor father-daughter relationship led to the exact opposite. These daughters were reported to have lower self-esteem and social competence. Additionally, they also had poor emotional regulation and communication adaptability. Girls who had absent fathers often grew up believing the paternal role was insignificant and undependable.

Another important thing worth noting is that women often chose romantic partners who displayed similar characteristics to their fathers. Insecurely attached women often carried around the adverse effects of their paternal relationship into their romantic relationships. Furthermore, fatherless women also viewed themselves as open, self-reliant, and capable of expressing their needs. Yet, these same women stayed in dysfunctional relationships. They were also more likely to remain silent in relationships for fear of pushing their partners away. They want to be dominant in the relationship but often get involved with men who fulfill stereotypical gender roles.

SIX HUMAN NEEDS

Anthony Robbins created the concept of six human needs. Robbins believed that happiness and success could be achieved if the six basic human needs are met. The first four needs are what he considered *needs of the personality*, while the last two are *needs of the soul*. The needs of the personality are the things that help define success and achievement. The spirit's needs are the needs that provide the base for a sense of fulfillment and joy.

The four needs of the personality are:

- **Certainty**—The need to have safety, comfort, predictability, and consistency
- **Uncertainty/Variety**—The need to have a challenge, variety, and adventure
- **Significance**—The need to have a sense of importance and worthiness
- **Love/Connection**—The need to feel connected, approved of and loved by other people

The needs of the spirit are:

- **Growth**—The need for constant stimulation necessary for intellectual, emotional, and spiritual growth
- **Contribution**—The need to serve and protect other individuals

People have different priorities over these needs. The way a person ranks them is also telling of who they are as individuals. If *variety* is your priority, you may partake in a lot of risky behavior just to get that adrenaline kicking. However, that also means that you're not afraid of challenges or meeting new people. If *significance* is one of your top two, then you crave recognition, whether it's to be seen or heard. Unfortunately, suppose you don't receive enough of the validation you need. As a result, you may surround yourself with people you view as less skilled or accomplished so that your abilities are highlighted. If *connection/love* is what you need most, you believe love is a wonderful gift life has to offer. This need will lead you to have rewarding relationships. The downside is that it may cause you to self-sacrifice just to keep a relationship. If *growth* is what you value, you are always trying to become a better version of yourself. You perform well at your job, but you move on to other things as soon as you've reached your maximum potential. Remember to relax. If *contribution* is your top need, you want to make a big difference in the community and always help others. However, you may often forget to help those closest to you because you're too busy helping strangers.

These six needs are quite paradoxical to each other. For example, more uncertainty results in less certainty. Significance and love/connection may also contradict each other. More growth may also result in less contribution. Nonetheless, how you rank these needs may reveal what kind of attachment you have.

YOUR WOUNDS AND YOUR NEEDS

To fully understand why the needs you perceive to be a priority are what you consider to be the most important, you first need to look at your core wounds. What needs were unmet during your childhood that you still carry today? What do you think your core wounds are? For example, if you believe you are unworthy, you might gravitate towards the need for significance. If you think to yourself, "Why would anyone love me?" there's a huge chance your unmet need could be love and connection.

Imagine Joan, an Anxious-Avoidant. Her parents were incredibly supportive during her childhood but often traveled for work. So, while they provided for her emotional needs, they weren't physically present all the time. This kind of behavior caused Joan to develop a fear of abandonment every time her parents left. What need do you think Joan resonates strongly with? If your answer is certainty, then you are entirely correct. As a kid, Joan felt that her parents lacked consistency. Sometimes they were there, and sometimes they were not. Therefore, she grew up valuing consistency and security. Then, she meets a guy named Robert. She and Robert hit it off right away, and soon they started dating. One day, Robert had a busy day at work and forgot to call Joan as soon as he got home, even though he promised to do so. When Robert failed to keep his promise, Joan's behavioral system caused her to engage in protest behavior. Remember that she values consistency, and when Robert didn't call her, she perceived this as a threat. As an adult, Joan needed consistency, security, and predictability in a relationship to reassure her that Robert would not abandon her.

TRAUMA AND ITS ROLE IN THE DEVELOPMENT OF YOUR ATTACHMENT STYLE

Aside from your unmet needs affecting your attachments, trauma also plays a big role in the development of your attachment style. Trauma is the most damaging factor in an attachment relationship. A healthy childhood meant the individual would grow up with the capacity of creating meaningful and secure relationships and positive self-esteem. Conversely, children who grew up bearing childhood trauma may have impaired social and emotional development. An example would be the absence of certain emotions like empathy and remorse. Another example would be having trouble creating and maintaining relationships. Aside from trauma affecting your attachment style, it even goes as far as manifesting physical and mental health issues.

In a study by Erozkan (2016), it was discovered that childhood trauma had a significant correlation with attachment styles. For securely attached individuals, they indicated a negative relationship with abuse and neglect. However, insecurely attached individuals stipulated a positive relationship with abuse and neglect. These results found that victims of abuse (physical, sexual, or emotional) and neglect (physical or emotional) usually developed insecure attachment styles. Furthermore, children immersed in neglectful and abusive environments were likely to manifest a disorganized attachment. Insecure attachment in children also occurs when they suffer from interpersonal abuse because it adversely affects their psychological development and internal working models. Erozkan concluded that negative childhood experiences had long-term negative effects on the development of both the physiological and mental health of an individual.

While researchers agree that trauma affects attachment styles, the concept of "attachment-related traumas" has also been introduced. It's been suggested that there are four types of attachment-related traumas. The first type is *attachment disruptions*, wherein there is an unanticipated and/or prolonged separation between the attachment figure and the individual, but no plans of reconnection are made. The second type is when the child is a victim of sexual abuse where the attachment figure is the perpetrator. The third type is when the child suffers from the attachment figure's loss. The fourth and final type is *attachment injuries* or wounds that emerge when the attachment figure abandons the child.

ENMESHMENT TRAUMA

Enmeshment trauma is another trauma that may cause children to become insecurely attached. *Enmeshment* occurs when there are no clear roles and boundaries set in a family. You would even consider it the opposite of abandonment. When parents project all their needs through their child, the child is forced to give up their sense of self to fulfill their parents' needs. Suppose a child is faced with one enmeshed parent and one emotionally unavailable parent. In that case, ultimately, the child believes that they are loved by their parents not because they are their children but because of what they can offer for their parents' self-esteem. Therefore, the child grows up avoiding a close relationship with others and being taken advantage of again. They fear that intimacy will just force them to suppress their emotional needs. Some victims of enmeshment trauma deny having emotional needs because they have never had the opportunity to explore their needs.

There are three types of enmeshed parents: romanticized, helicopter, and incapacitated. A *romanticized parent* uses their children as an alternative to an adult friend. They often derive their happiness from their children, whom they force to become their emotional support. Sometimes, the romanticized parent will use guilt to manipulate their children into doing what they want. The next type, *helicopter parent*, is something we're all familiar with. The helicopter parent is over-involved in their child's life. They will do whatever it takes to protect their child from harm and even go as far as making decisions for their child. Unfortunately, the child starts to believe that they live their lives for their parents and have lost their core self because of what the parent does. The last one is the *incapacitated parent*. This parent is either physically, mentally, or sometimes financially incapacitated. Sometimes, the parent suffers from an addiction of some sort and cannot fulfill the role of a caregiver. In this scenario, the child, usually the eldest, steps up to take the role of the parent. This means that the child will begin doing household responsibilities and, if they have siblings, helping to raise them. When a situation like that occurs, it is called parentification, which is also a form of abuse.

THE FOUR TRAUMA RESPONSES

As we've discussed, childhood trauma is a heavy burden we carry into adulthood. Your biggest enemy when dealing with trauma is the lack of self-awareness. Trauma comes in various forms, so some people may not be too quick to realize it. When faced with a complex situation, most people are familiar with the fight-or-flight response. However, there are also other recognized trauma responses. There are four known trauma responses: *fight, flight, freeze*, and *fawn*. Fight and flight are the most well-known trauma responses, while the freeze and fawn responses are the least known. When done correctly, it is still possible to exhibit a trauma response, but this time in a healthier manner.

A fight response is usually made out of self-preservation. Examples of an unhealthy fight response could be lashing out, throwing objects, or getting into a physical altercation. When done correctly, it is still possible to exhibit a fight response, but this time in a more productive way. When used positively, a fight response can help you set firm boundaries and become more assertive.

When faced with a confrontation, people who engage in a flight response would get up and leave the premises. However, there are other less subtle flight responses, such as avoiding the situation as soon as you sense conflict arising or self-sabotaging. However, a healthy flight response can help you find the courage to leave toxic relationships and avoid physically dangerous situations.

The third trauma response, freeze, happens when a person is incapable of either fleeing or fighting. Instead, they are glued to their place due to the overwhelming amount of fear they feel. This can be overtly observed when a person dissociates, isolates, or zones out. When practiced in a healthier way, a freeze response can be perceived as mindfulness or awareness.

The last one, fawn, is the least-recognized trauma response, probably because it doesn't blatantly look like a trauma response. In times of conflict, people who have a fawn response resort to people-pleasing. Those who people-please during times of conflict often impose little to no boundaries. They will also go above and beyond other people to the point of self-betrayal. On the other hand, by setting healthy boundaries and with a bit of practice, a healthy fawn response can help you be more compassionate for people and become an active listener.

Depending on what attachment style you have, there are trauma responses you are more likely to engage in first. The primary trauma response for dismissive-avoidant people is flight. During an argument, their first course of action is to leave the room and get some space. Next to flight comes freeze. Instead of fleeing, they may just clam up and avoid talking about it, only for them to make passive-aggressive comments later on. Suppose these people continue to engage in flight or freeze. Over time, some pent-up anger will result in an outburst—a fight response. Dismissive-avoidant people are least likely to exhibit a fawn response because, as children, they learned how to put themselves first and self-soothe. Therefore, they are more self-oriented people.

Fearful-avoidant people, on the other hand, are big people-pleasers. As children, they had to learn to put other people's needs above their own, specifically their parents'. Due to the inconsistency they experienced from their parents as kids, they might also engage in a fight response. The third response they could have would be the flight response. But it would almost be impossible for a fearful-avoidant to exhibit a freeze response. Fearful-avoidant children could not afford to freeze. They struggled with trusting other people, so they usually had to find a way out of whatever situation they were in.

Anxious-avoidant people will also exhibit fawn as their knee-jerk trauma response. They believe that they will receive affection and prevent conflict or abandonment if they can please people. If not, they may respond to an argument by freezing instead because, in their mind, fighting or fleeing may lead to abandonment. The third response they exhibit would be fight. However, in this case, it doesn't mean a physical altercation. A fight response may mean engaging in protest behavior for anxious-avoidant people to try and get a reaction. Anxious-avoidant people are least likely to have a flight response because they associate fleeing with abandonment.

EMBRACING YOUR TRAUMA

Childhood trauma is something that you may carry with you until your death. Unfortunately, there is no way for us to go back in time and undo all the damage our parents caused us. That being said, the best way to deal with your trauma is to embrace it. Embracing your trauma is the first step to healing and understanding the self. You don't have to be so hard on yourself. Understand that you had no control over how you were treated as a child, so don't blame yourself for reacting the way you do in threatening situations. It's your brain's way of coping.

Do you know what the good thing is, though? Our brain is capable of changing. Your past doesn't have to define your present. By understanding what went wrong, you can remodel your brain to practice healthier coping mechanisms. I'm not saying this in a snotty, "Get over it" kind of way. I, and everybody else on this planet, have no right to dismiss what you went through or what you're still going through in life. All I'm saying is, there's hope for all of us. We are all capable of healing from our past. It's not just wishful thinking; it's science.

Think of trauma as a rock you carry in your pocket. Initially, the rock will be a heavy burden you have to carry. Its weight will also do a great job of reminding you of its existence. Over time, as you begin to heal and forgive yourself, the rock will start to seem lighter. Eventually, you might even forget about the rock's existence. Unfortunately, there might be days where you will remember its presence inside your pocket, but it won't be as heavy as it used to be. For you, it will be nothing more than a mere pebble.

3

WHAT IS YOUR ATTACHMENT STYLE?

John Bowlby was more interested in understanding the attachment in an infant-caregiver relationship. However, Cindy Hazan and Philip Shaver (1987) were among the first people to explore the possibility that the attachment styles Ainsworth identified were also possible in romantic relationships. They believed that if Bowlby's theory was also applicable to romantic relationships, then it was clear that attachment theory is both a biological and a social process. Although, if there was one thing they admitted in their study, it was that relationships are complex phenomena. It would be hard to formulate causations and predictions based on personalities alone. For example, they believed a secure partner might become *anxious* when paired with a dismissive-avoidant partner. Therefore, it is safe to say that our attachments are malleable and depend on the dynamics of each relationship. Despite the similarities between attachment theory in infant-caregiver relationships and romantic relationships, it wouldn't come as a surprise if the latter proved to be more complicated than the former. There are many more variables to consider in adult relationships, making attachment theory a very complex and challenging task to take on.

As we briefly discussed in the first chapter, there are four known attachment styles: secure, anxious-preoccupied, dismissive-avoidant, and fearful-avoidant. In this chapter, we will have a more in-depth discussion about the different attachment styles. We will define each attachment style and talk about its main characteristics. Furthermore, we will also discover whether gender influences your attachment style. You will also learn how to use your attachment style to your advantage. With this knowledge, you can build better relationships with your coworkers, friends, romantic partners, family members, and even your parents.

Bartholomew created a two-dimensional, four-category scheme to illustrate Bowlby's idea of the internal working models. She believed the four attachment patterns could be defined in two dimensions: a model of the self and a model of others. The model of the self could be related to the degree of anxiety, while the model of others could be related to the degree of closeness or avoidance in relationships. A more positive view of the self meant lower anxiety, whereas a more positive view of others meant lower avoidance in relationships.

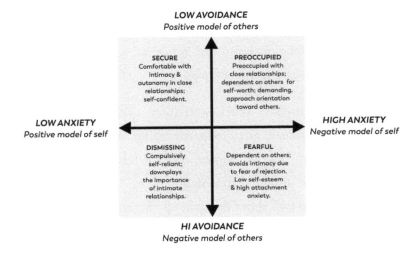

Bartholomew's two dimensional, four-prototype model of adult attachment

DISMISSIVE-AVOIDANT ATTACHMENT

Hazan and Shaver (1987) believed this statement was the best way to describe a dismissive-avoidant's feelings: "I am somewhat uncomfortable being close to others; I find it difficult to trust them completely, difficult to allow myself to depend on them. I am nervous when anyone gets too close, and often, romantic partners want me to be more intimate than I feel comfortable being."

In Hazan and Shaver's love quiz, dismissive-avoidant people deeply resonated with the following sentences:

- Intense romantic love is expected at the beginning of a relationship, but it rarely lasts forever.
- It's rare to find someone you can fall in love with.

- I am more independent and self-sufficient than most people; I can get along quite well by myself.
- You have to watch out when dealing with most people; they will hurt, ignore, or reject you if it suits their purposes.

Their study discovered that participants who were described as dismissive tended to prioritize work over relationships. They believed that work brought greater happiness in their lives compared to relationships. If they had to choose between career success and relationship success, they would choose the former.

Going back to enmeshment trauma, when children grow up in the hands of a romanticized parent, they are likely to become dismissive-avoidant. During their childhood, their parents used them as an "emotional punching bag." Now that they are adults, they fear getting too close to people lest they fall into this role once again. They are wary of commitment and feel suffocated in intimate relationships. They also possess unwarranted self-confidence because they were so used to being placed on a pedestal with minimal effort on their part. An inflated ego is another characteristic of a dismissive-avoidant.

Dismissive-avoidant people tend to idealize their childhood and their relationship with their parents. They have little access to childhood memories to avoid bringing up negative feelings that they suppressed throughout their childhood. Though they claimed they had a good relationship with their parents, they mentioned negative descriptions of their parents, such as critical, disinterested, and rejecting. And even when they brought up memories that others would consider harmful, they still downplayed the emotional intensity. In contrast, dismissive-avoidant people were less likely to idealize their romantic relationships.

When asked, dismissive-avoidants are more likely to claim never having been in love and believe their romantic relationships were rather dull. They tend to dismiss romantic relationships and prefer their independence. They think that entering a relationship meant giving up their independence and freedom. As children, they were often held back from expressing negative or positive feelings. Because of this, they developed a fear of trusting others. Their need for independence and control is their way of protecting themselves from any emotional disappointment, such as caregiver or romantic partner unavailability. When avoidant individuals engage in sexual activities, they tend to disconnect their emotions from the act to avoid closeness. They may even avoid sexual activities altogether.

There are easy ways to tell whether a person has a dismissive-avoidant personality. The following sentences are some common characteristics of dismissive-avoidant people:

- When relied on by their partners, they become overwhelmed and withdraw.
- They believe entering a relationship will only cut off their freedom.
- As much as possible, they will avoid self-disclosure.
- They neither ask for nor accept help from others.
- They are highly independent.
- They are constantly looking for "someone better," even though they are already in a relationship.

- They often use deactivating strategies to keep their partners at arm's length.

Deactivating strategies are actions or behaviors that seek to shut off the attachment system to avoid closeness and deny attachment needs. Engaging in deactivating strategies is one common characteristic that dismissive-avoidant people share. For example, they may send mixed signals to their partner. They claim they are not ready to commit and refuse to say, "I love you," but stay with their partner for many months (or years) and imply that they have feelings for them. Another example of a deactivating strategy is displaying utter disinterest in their partner's personal life and putting in no effort to get to know them.

For example, imagine an eight-year-old boy, Pete. Pete's parents have high-paying jobs that require them to go on a lot of work trips and stay late in the office. Instead of growing up with his parents, Pete grew up being cared for by a nanny. Thus, he spent a lot of time alone. Pete was a quiet kid and did well academically in school, so his parents believed he was an independent kid who didn't need to be validated. Consequently, Pete grew up being highly self-sufficient and refuses to seek comfort from others. Even when Pete struggles with whatever issue he is faced with, he tries to do everything independently because he doesn't trust people to deliver on their promises, just like how his parents never bothered to check up on his needs.

However, do not think dismissive-avoidant people are the wrong partners. Distancing themselves is their brain's way of protecting themselves from pain. During their childhood, they were constantly let down by their parents. As a result, they believe that vulnerability will always lead to disappointment and that they can only truly rely on themselves. Expecting rejection in times of discomfort, they did not try to risk seeking comfort from their parents. Dismissive-avoidants distance themselves from other people because being alone was the only childhood memory that held a positive memory. A dismissive-avoidant adult has been molded by years and years of shutting down as a form of defense. Despite being in an overtly safe and comfortable environment, the individual's internal working models will see it as a threat.

Based on the traits mentioned above, if a considerable majority of those apply to you, you may be a dismissive-avoidant.

FEARFUL-AVOIDANT ATTACHMENT

According to the work of Kim Bartholomew (1990), there are two types of avoidance. She argued that one type of avoidance was focused on defensiveness and self-sufficiency, while the other held a conscious fear of expected rejection. The first type is the one we previously discussed, dismissive-avoidant. The second type is the fearful-avoidant attachment style. Bartholomew suggested that describing avoidance as a single category would be an issue. She pointed out another group of avoidant individuals who are more fearful of close relationships and less dismissive of them. The fearful-avoidant is more conscious of the need for intimacy and yet anticipates rejection and disappointment from their peers.

Bartholomew found that fearful-avoidant individuals have the following characteristics:

- Great susceptibility to loneliness and depression
- Believes they are undeserving of love and support from their peers
- Struggles with autonomy and intimacy
- Steers clear of closeness to reduce the potential pain from disappointment
- Dependent on others for a positive view of self
- Hypersensitive to social approval

Bartholomew and Horrowitz (1991) found that fearful-avoidant individuals held self-disclosure, intimacy, and reliance on others in negative regard. They also observed that fearful-avoidants were less likely to use a romantic partner as a secure base in times of distress. Furthermore, these individuals also possessed a tendency to be compliant in close relationships.

Going back to Bartholomew's model, it can be observed that fearful-avoidants have a negative view of both the self *and* others. Like the anxious individual, they desire to form intimate bonds with other people. However, they dismiss close relationships to protect themselves from pain because of past experiences and negative expectations.

The fearful-avoidant adult is a mix of the anxious and the dismissive. Hence, they are caught in a constant battle of approach avoidance. This means they are quick to shift from being emotionally available to emotionally distant. According to Bartholomew's four-category model, they also exhibit high anxiety and high avoidance as they hold a negative view of both others and themselves.

While the dismissive-avoidant child was not allowed to express their emotions openly, the fearful-avoidant child was faced with the opposite. Parents of these children may have openly expressed negative feelings towards and in front of their children. This caused the child to fear them. But because they are also the primary attachment figure, the child is also attached to them. As a result, the child develops a disorganized attachment to the parent. Dutton et al. (1994) found that men with a fearful-avoidant style had high levels of chronic anxiety and anger. Fearful-avoidants also had higher trauma and dissociation scores.

Findings from a study by Favez and Tissot (2019) discovered that fearful avoidance had a direct link with sexuality. Fearful-avoidant women were found to have a higher number of partners over a lifetime, whereas men had more positive responses to sexual solicitations. As we've discussed, people with such characteristics have high anxiety and avoidance. The heightened anxiety may lead to the individual craving closeness with a partner through sexual activities. The high level of avoidance may also lead the individual to break the bond that was formed. Due to the constant battle between approach and avoidance, it may result in compulsive sexual behaviors. Results also proved that higher fearful avoidance meant lower sexual satisfaction.

Fearful avoidants are a bit different when it comes to friendships. They're what we would call hot and cold. When they're "hot," they're surprisingly one of the greatest friends you could ask for. They're attentive and present in the situation. Because of their hypersensitivity, they can easily tell when their friends are feeling off, making them very sensitive to their friends' emotions. However, because fearful-avoidants struggle with setting boundaries, they sometimes spend too much time and emotional energy on their friendships. They feel that they are responsible for their friends' feelings. As a result, they get exhausted from all the emotional energy they gave away. When this happens, the fearful-avoidant will slowly withdraw. Then, they'll suddenly disappear for long periods without communicating with their friends. Their friends, who have different attachment styles, will take it personally and give the fearful-avoidant a tough time. In turn, the fearful-avoidant will feel guilty and withdraw even more. If they can't learn to set boundaries, they will have trouble balancing all their emotional relationships. If you happen to be the friend of a fearful-avoidant, don't take it personally when they disappear for days and don't reach out. They are withdrawing because they feel emotionally spent and overwhelmed. It certainly has nothing to do with you.

The fearful-avoidant attachment is usually created due to the parents' emotional inconsistency. Many inconsistencies may stem from personality disorders or addictions, or the parents may rely on their children for emotional support but refuse to reciprocate. Even the sexual dysfunctions found in fearful-avoidants have been theoretically linked to some form of psychological trauma. In some cases, the parents may have been abusive, too. When children are raised in volatile environments, they become hypersensitive to social cues. No matter what situation they are in, their brains will always be on the lookout for the slightest change in the emotion, tone, or body language of whoever they are with.

For example, we have Jade. Jade's father suffered from alcoholism. Because of this, she had to constantly be careful around her father to avoid his violent outbursts. However, when her father was sober, he was lovely and caring towards Jade. Her father's alcoholism caused her parents to fight constantly. Jade was an only child and became her mother's emotional punching bag. She would continuously vent her issues to her daughter, but whenever Jade needed comfort, her mother would often dismiss and downplay her needs. Over time, Jade realized her father was the only one who did not undermine her needs. However, because he was drunk and violent most days, she had also grown to fear him. Because of the volatility she experienced in her household, she became wary of connecting with others. Deep down, she recognizes that she has needs that should be met, but she dismisses them because of the fear of being hurt and disappointed.

Let's look at another situation where a person developed a fearful-avoidant attachment. Here we have Alyssa. Alyssa's parents divorced when she was nine, and now she lives with her mom. Alyssa's mom is very critical of her and often pressures her to excel in school. In the privacy of their home, Alyssa's mom often hurls negative comments at her whenever she does something deemed incompetent in her mother's eyes. However, when they are out in public, her mother often compliments her when others are around. Due to this, Alyssa had a confusing relationship with her mother. On the one hand, she knew her mother loved her because of how she spoke about her when other people were around. On the other hand, when it was just the two of them, she never failed to belittle her accomplishments and undermine her struggles in school.

If all of the things we discussed about the anxious-avoidant style apply to you, then it's likely that you have a fearful-avoidant attachment style.

ANXIOUS-PREOCCUPIED ATTACHMENT

If you have an anxious-preoccupied attachment style, then you may have high anxiety and low avoidance. This means you hold a negative view of the self but have a positive view of others. In Hazan and Shaver's study, they believed that the following statement best described the anxious individual, "I find that others are reluctant to get as close as I would like. I often worry that my partner doesn't really love me or want to stay with me. I want to merge completely with another person, and this desire sometimes scares people away."

Some of the common characteristics of an anxious-preoccupied individual can also be described in the following sentences:

- I tend to doubt myself more than most of my peers.
- I find that not everyone is as committed to a long-term relationship as I am.
- I believe people don't put in the effort to get to know me deeper.
- I find it very easy to fall in love with someone.

Anxious-preoccupied individuals seek a relationship with an intense, burning passion. However, whenever they are in a relationship, they find that their partner is unwilling to reciprocate with the same intensity and desire they seek. Furthermore, anxious individuals derive their self-worth from their romantic partner's approval, so they are huge people-pleasers more often than not.

Anxious people have high levels of *intimacy anger* (Dutton et al., 1994). Intimacy anger occurs when the individual presents an adverse reaction when attachment cues emerge. High levels of intimacy anger are directly related to their negative view of the self and their desire to meet their emotional needs. Furthermore, they found that anxious women have an intense fear of abandonment in romantic relationships. Therefore, they possess high levels of anger and jealousy.

Enmeshment trauma may also cause adults to develop an anxious-preoccupied attachment style. Their core wound revolves around their parents' conditional love. As children, they only received affection when they did something that pleased their parents. Thus, they believe that they are unlovable individuals and have abandonment issues. In tune with this, anxious-preoccupied individuals are more likely to enter abusive or codependent relationships.

In a separate study, Henderson et al. (2005) also found that anxious people are torn between the need to receive affection from others and fear rejection from not having their needs realized. They also discovered that anxious-preoccupied individuals were more likely to fall into abusive relationships and stay there. Because they tend to idealize their romantic partners, anxious people are more likely to excuse their partner's abusive behavior and tolerate the abuse. They have unrealistic expectations that their abusive partners will change for the better and stick around waiting for them to change.

Protest behavior is something we defined in the first chapter. This is another kind of behavior that anxious individuals will engage in. Aside from those previously mentioned, there is another example of protest behavior that these individuals use. In situations of abusive relationships, anxious-preoccupied women often threaten to leave the relationship as a means of scaring their partner into changing their abusive behavior.

One characteristic that anxious individuals share with fearful-avoidants is their hypersensitivity to social cues and body language. When the anxious-preoccupied senses that there is a slight shift in the relationship, their attachment system becomes activated. When the system is triggered, the individual will engage in *activating strategies*. Dismissive-avoidants engage in *deactivating strategies* that aim to turn off their attachment needs. On the other hand, anxious-preoccupied people engage in activating strategies that compel you to reestablish a connection with a romantic partner. Examples of activating strategies include:

- Remembering only your partner's good qualities
- Idealizing them and believing your abilities pale in comparison to theirs
- Emotional dumping on friends of partners
- Engaging in clinging behaviors

Anxious-preoccupied individuals fear loneliness, so they are quick to jump from one relationship into another. They may even use sexuality to intensify their relationship with others, even if there is no sexual desire, to avoid rejection. There is nothing wrong with entering a new relationship after you've ended a previous one. However, people should always give themselves proper time to truly understand what they want and need. Additionally, suppose the previous relationship was unhealthy. In that case, it is important to give themselves time to heal from the wounds from the old relationship lest they bring those wounds into the new relationship and cause more issues to arise.

Like fearful-avoidants, a person may have an anxious-preoccupied attachment when there is an inconsistency in parenthood. Let's use Tony as an example. Tony's dad was always present, supporting, and loving. On the other hand, Tony's mother was a workaholic and spent a lot of time away from home. Due to his mother spending a lot of time away from home, a constant need to be close to his mother will arise in him. Eventually, he will engage in activating strategies to ensure his mother spends more time with him and less time away from home. Over time, Tony becomes so focused on the activating strategies that he never learned how to self-soothe. Self-soothing is essential because it allows us to deal with frustrations more rationally. In romantic relationships, not knowing how to self-soothe prevents us from facing the problem. We become too focused on coming up with strategies that stop the partner from leaving the relationship.

If you resonate with the many qualities of an anxious-preoccupied, then you have this attachment style.

SECURE ATTACHMENT

Secure attachment is defined as having a positive view of the self and others. They also rank low on anxiety and avoidance. Securely attached people:

- Agree that romantic feelings may wax and wane over time, but they can also be as intense as they were at the beginning of the relationship
- Believe romantic love never fades
- Believe people are generally kind and mean well
- Are accepting of their partner despite their flaws
- Feel comfortable depending on their partner and vice versa
- Are comfortable with intimacy in close relationships

Generally speaking, secure individuals have positive beliefs about love. When in romantic relationships, secure individuals also experience higher relationship satisfaction and effective conflict resolution. They described their relationship experiences as happy, trusting, and affectionate. They can create bonds with their romantic partners without losing their autonomy as well. Furthermore, secure individuals have a positive view of sexual activities, which leads to them enjoying sexual activities and the intimacy that comes with them.

A secure attachment is formed from a positive childhood experience. When individuals have emotionally supportive and available relationships, they learn that their needs matter. They don't view vulnerability as a threat to their emotional safety. Due to these factors, they have good self-esteem and are not afraid of exploring their environment.

As mentioned at the beginning of this chapter, Hazan and Shaver felt that relationships and attachments are complex phenomena that need to be studied intensively. With that being said, a securely attached individual can help their insecurely attached partner shift to have a more secure attachment. Our attachment styles are malleable, and we can transition into a more secure attachment.

Can't remember the attachment styles?
Download my attachment style "cheat sheet" by going to
MasterYourAttachmentStyle.com/CheatSheet

SEXUAL ORIENTATION AND ATTACHMENT STYLES

A large majority of the studies about attachment theory are focused on heterosexual couples. However, over the years, more and more researchers have slowly begun to explore the correlation between attachment styles and sexual orientation.

We have learned that our childhood experiences shape our attachment styles. Because sexual orientation is mostly only fully realized after childhood, it is unlikely that sexual orientation leads to a negative parent-child relationship. Ridge and Feeney (1998) concluded from their study that for gay males and lesbians, parental history did not influence their attachment style. They also found that secure gay males were more likely to open up early on in a relationship. In contrast, secure lesbians had a positive relationship with their mothers both before and after coming out.

As we go through life, we are always trying to figure out our identities. Our sexual orientation, therefore, is a vital component in identity development. Lesbians comfortable expressing their sexual orientation were found to have a secure attachment style (Alessi et al., 2011). This means that a securely attached individual will be more comfortable accepting and disclosing their sexual orientation. Furthermore, securely attached lesbians will have better identity development compared to their peers with insecure attachments.

In contrast, Landolt et al. (2004) discovered that gender nonconforming behavior directly correlated with maternal, paternal, and peer rejection in gay men. *Gender nonconformity* is when people refuse to conform to gender roles. For example, boys are expected to be tough and hide their emotions. When boys go against this norm and, instead, are very open with their emotions, then they are engaging in gender-nonconforming behavior. Boys who grew up experiencing gender nonconformity were likely to deal with paternal and peer rejection. Peer rejection brought about attachment anxiety and avoidance in adulthood. Paternal rejection also had a direct association with attachment avoidance in adulthood. This could be because some fathers have trouble accepting gender nonconforming behavior in their sons. In turn, some gay men find it difficult to create trusting, intimate relationships in adulthood. Gender nonconformity was also observed to influence an anxious attachment in adulthood. Since gender nonconformity may lead to peer rejection, it causes anxiety in individuals.

In a separate study, Brown and Trevethan (2010) also found that shame, internalized homophobia, and attachment styles in gay men were closely related. Gay men who were currently in a relationship were observed to have a less anxious attachment compared to gay men who were currently single. Furthermore, insecure attachments and internalized homophobia were plausible predictors of shame.

LIMERENCE

Limerence is a term probably not everybody is familiar with. Dr. Dorothy Tennov coined it in 1979 in her book, *Love and Limerence*. According to Dr. Tennov, *limerence* is a state of infatuation with a person, or your limerent object (LO), to the point of obsessiveness. When *limerence* occurs, the person's emotions or behavior controls them, instead of them being in control of their reactions. The person, called the limerent, has a deep craving for the LO to reciprocate their intense feelings. Usually, it happens when we least expect it. Furthermore, some people don't experience it at all, or they might only experience it once or twice in their life.

Here are some of the characterizations of limerence:

- **Obsessive-compulsive thoughts about the limerent object.** You might describe this as being "madly in love." Dr. Tennov says that about 85% or more of the limerent's day is spent thinking about the LO when limerence occurs. They might spend hours thinking about their LO's voice, laugh, or how much fun they had with them.

- **Exaggerated fantasies about the limerent object.** In a way, this coincides with the first one, but there is a slight difference. Here, the limerent is consumed by thoughts about their future with the LO, even though they hardly know them. For example, they've only gone on two dates with the person, and the limerent believes that person is "The One." They start conjuring fantasies about their future with their LO, like their wedding and how many children they'll have. In the end, it disrupts everyday life because their fantasies so consume the limerent that they are unable to focus on other things.

- **Fear of rejection.** Here, the limerent worries about what the LO thinks about them. When they are in the presence of their LO, they display bouts of introversion because they feel intimidated and are afraid of messing up. They might even display physical symptoms when in the presence of their LO, like sweating, heart palpitations, and dizziness.

- **Unreasonable amounts of hopefulness.** Even though the relationship has ended or the LO has expressed their intentions of not wanting to date, the limerent is unreasonably hopeful even after many years have passed. For example, they will go out of their way to manipulate a situation to bump into their LO so they can have a conversation. They might spend the next few years (or worse, their whole life) pining for this "soulmate" that they lost.

- **Overly idealizing their limerent object.** Here, the limerent will put their LO on an extremely high pedestal. They will dismiss all their LO's negative traits and overamplify their positive traits. Idealizing your partner is normal to some extent during the honeymoon phase. With limerence, the limerent refuses to acknowledge the red flags and overlook all their disruptive habits.

Limerence may happen because the limerent has a deeply unmet need, and they think their LO is the only source for that need to be met. It's kind of like that saying, "We don't know what we've been missing until it arrives." The limerent may perceive something missing from their life, such as a person they can have deep conversations with. When they get a taste of it, they perceive it to be a rarity, so they latch onto it. Hazan and Shaver (1987) found that anxious-preoccupied people saw love as a desire for reciprocation, an emotional rollercoaster, and an extreme sexual attraction to their partner. This bears rather similar qualities to limerence. Anxious-preoccupied people are more prone to experience limerence compared to other attachment styles. They suggest that the difference between love and limerence can be distinguished through the secure and anxious-preoccupied attachments. Securely attached individuals are comfortable giving or receiving affection from other people. They also feel secure in handling their romantic relationships. On the contrary, anxious people feel as though the relationship is unrequited. Because it's unrequited, they crave reciprocation.

RELATIONSHIPS AND YOUR ATTACHMENT

There's a lot of power in being actively aware of your attachment style. With the knowledge you possess, you can use it to navigate your way around your romantic and non-romantic relationships. Not only that, it may offer you a look into your friends' and partner's attachment styles, too.

Acknowledging your trauma is one thing, but actively turning off your defense mechanisms is another. Working towards becoming a better and more secure version of yourself is a task you must be willing to work on.

For example, you may catch yourself in situations where you felt guilty for asking for help from a friend. Well, don't! Tell your brain there's no shame in asking for help. The more you condition your brain into thinking more positively, the less likely it will be to bring up your core wounds and use them against you.

Another example we are all familiar with is "Facebook stalking." The act of stalking an ex-lover or an old friend is a product of our attachment style, too. During a breakup with a partner or a falling out with a friend, the person is removed from our life. Usually, anxious-preoccupied individuals are more likely to demand reconnection after a separation and, therefore, succumb to Facebook stalking. After a falling out, the individual's internal working model is in great distress. This may cause them to monitor the former friend or partner's activities. However, this is counterintuitive. Facebook stalking just prevents a person from healing. If a person can't heal and accept that some relationships just don't work out, moving on becomes a more challenging task, too.

Furthermore, understanding your attachment style helps you understand your life experiences better. With attachment theory, you may begin to realize how your past was a traumatic experience that you went through but weren't aware of. Remember our example with Jayden and Tommy? If Jayden hadn't started exploring how his past trauma affected who he is now, he probably would have ended the relationship with Tommy. But because he understood that Tommy's presence in his life had nothing to do with his lashing out, he was able to save the relationship. So you see, understanding your core self may even help you save relationships.

When you start recognizing that your attachment behaviors are only trying to protect you from the same kind of pain you experienced during your childhood, it's easier to forgive yourself. Furthermore, it will be easier for you to understand the motivation behind some of your friends' or partners' actions.

Our traumatic experiences and attachments heavily influence even our core beliefs. These traumatic events affect how we see ourselves, other people, and the world. Suppose we want to work on transitioning into having a secure attachment. In that case, we must be willing to consider the possibility of reframing our core beliefs to react less defensively whenever we form relationships with others.

4

OVERCOMING LIMITING BELIEFS

So far, we've covered various topics surrounding attachment theory. We've learned who the proponents of attachment theory are. We've also explored why attachments matter in children and what happens when parents don't provide good quality caregiving. Lastly, we've also had a more in-depth discussion of the four different attachment styles—their common traits, the probable cause behind their development, and their core beliefs.

In this chapter, we will talk about your limiting beliefs. It will shed some light on your beliefs and how your attachment style has shaped these beliefs. Furthermore, we will discuss how overcoming your limiting beliefs will guide you towards reprogramming your attachment style.

WHAT LIMITING BELIEFS ARE

A lot of the decisions we make are guided by our core beliefs. Maybe as a child, you were bold and fearless. However, as you transitioned into adulthood, you were introduced to rules and customs about how you should behave, react, and be, which molded your core beliefs. These beliefs influence our thoughts, feelings, and behavior. While some of our beliefs are well-intentioned and benefit us a great deal, we also have beliefs that hinder us from achieving our greatest potential. This is what we call our *limiting beliefs*.

Limiting beliefs are beliefs you hold to be true that restrict you in some way. These could revolve around how you think about yourself, how you think about others, or how you think about the world around you. For example, your limiting beliefs can stop you from applying for your dream job or from doing something extreme, like skydiving. Supposedly, our limiting beliefs are our mind's way of protecting us from struggles, disappointment, or heartbreak.

There are three types of limiting beliefs that impede your growth as an individual:

- **Limiting beliefs about yourself**—These beliefs stop you from doing what you want because you believe there is something inherently wrong with you. Similarly, you might have an overly optimistic belief about yourself that could result in an inflated ego.
- **Limiting beliefs about others**—You believe that people are generally ill-intentioned and are only out to pull you

down. Contrarily, you may also have too much faith in others that might also allow them to take advantage of you.

- **Limiting beliefs about the world**—You have a belief that the world is out to get you and that it will never give you what you want. On the other hand, you may have a highly romanticized view of the world, which may also harm you along the way.

The truth is, none of these beliefs is completely accurate. These are just false realities conjured by your brain that keep you in a pessimistic state of mind. A study published in July 2020 found that adults generate over six thousand thoughts per day. Given that statistic, imagine how much we're holding ourselves back if we let our limiting beliefs take control of our minds and our actions.

HOW OUR LIMITING BELIEFS ARE FORMED

It's tough to pinpoint one particular factor responsible for our core beliefs simply because there's more than one influence on them. Many factors influence the formation of our limiting beliefs. It may come from our childhood, the environment we grew up in, or our life experiences.

When a child experiences a traumatic event, no matter how many years pass, that event will forever be embedded in their memory. Furthermore, what the brain will remember the most is what they did to stay safe at that moment. The thought process behind that action will eventually repeat itself over and over well into adulthood. If the traumatic event isn't realized, the individual will suffer the negative consequences of it. If individuals fail to address the traumatic events or the negative consequences, they might struggle to make better choices late into adulthood. Do you realize how damaging that is? Imagine being 50 and still letting your past dictate your current life choices.

Our beliefs may also be an extension of our family's belief system. Within a family unit, there are roles each family member must fulfill. Your parents may have had beliefs that they enforced on you as well, or they had phrases that you heard repeatedly growing up that have projected themselves into your thoughts. These beliefs may also be influenced by culture and religion, such as children were never allowed to question people of authority, including their parents. Another example could be that the eldest children in the family must help out in taking care of their younger siblings. Regardless, these expectations and roles impacted your beliefs about relationships, career, work, and dreams.

Another factor would be our life experiences. As we grow older, we go through many ups and downs. Failed relationships may cause us to rethink our stance on love and relationships. If a person gets cheated on more than once, they might eventually view love as a negative emotion.

Ultimately, I believe all of these factors boil down to the emotions we experienced at that moment. Think about it. So many people have different stories, yet our limiting beliefs are similar. How could that be? That's because, as children, we were incapable of fully comprehending the emotions we felt. As a result, our brain translated it into a core belief. That being said, it's impossible to overcome our limiting beliefs without dealing with the underlying emotion behind that belief.

COMMON LIMITING BELIEFS AND HOW THEY AFFECT YOUR LIFE

There are many limiting beliefs a person may have. Some can be described in the following statements:

- *"I am not worthy."*
- *"I deserved that because I am not a good person."*
- *"There's no point in trying this because I know I'm going to fail."*
- *"No one really cares about me anyway."*
- *"What's the point in starting a relationship? I'm just going to get hurt anyway."*
- *"If I don't achieve (milestone) by (age), I'm never going to be successful."*
- *"Why would anyone hire me? I don't have enough experience for this."*
- *"If I show who I really am, people might judge me for it."*
- *"They'll never want me because I'm not pretty enough."*
- *"It's so hard to find a connection with other people who understand my humor and my personality."*

I know many of us have said at least one thing from that list to ourselves. What we don't realize is how damaging it is to our self-esteem and our perception of the world. Have you ever come across an opportunity you wanted to take but didn't because you were too afraid of failing? Did you ever regret not taking it? If you did, do you see how big of an influence your belief has on your choices? Do you realize how much potential you have if you stopped listening to your limiting beliefs?

The most common limiting belief is believing you're not capable of doing something because you're just going to fail. You're not even giving yourself a chance to try it out. How would you know you can't do it if you didn't even try? Or let's say you did, and you failed at it the first time. Are you just going to let that mistake dictate your choices? There is no such thing as "I can't do this" because people can always do things. People rarely get things right the first time, so don't be too hard on yourself if you had to repeat it seven times before you could do it. How can we learn from our mistakes if we are perfect every single time? Trust me, I've had my fair share of mistakes, too, in the kitchen, in relationships, and life.

I think another reason behind many missed opportunities is believing we don't have the time for it. In a way, if we work 40 hours a week, maybe we really won't be too keen on going out and doing something. I get that. But if you repeatedly tell yourself you don't have the time, this will eventually be your reality. The next thing we know, life has passed us by. This time, we have no more time to try out a new hobby or spend time with our loved ones.

There are many opportunities in life that we often allow to pass by. These could have been job opportunities, adventures, or even people. All because we told ourselves we weren't good enough for it. This is the most damaging limiting belief there is because it's fundamentally harmful to your self-esteem. The more you tell yourself that you're not good enough, the more you start to believe it. In the words of a Never Shout Never song, "You're only as tall as your heart will let you be, and you're only as small as the world will make you seem." You are always good enough for whatever comes your way. You are here. You exist. You matter. If it's hard for you to believe in those words, how can you expect the world to believe you?

Like I've said before, our limiting beliefs affect our lives and our relationships. Suppose you had parents that were very critical of you. They critiqued your talent, your hobbies, and maybe even your appearance. As a result, you develop these limiting beliefs based on what they said about you. When you grow up and enter relationships, you are more prone to date people who are also very critical of you because of these limiting beliefs. You know you deserve better, but your subconscious is so used to being judged that it's hard to believe that's not actually who you are. Another situation could be if you had a partner who cheated on you. You may start thinking you can't trust your next partner because you're too afraid of the cycle repeating itself.

YOUR LIMITING BELIEFS AND YOUR ATTACHMENT STYLE

In chapter 3, we discussed the four different types of attachment styles. You see, our limiting beliefs coincide with our attachment style. Have you noticed some of the statements we mentioned can be associated with an attachment style?

For example, "I am not worthy" and "They'll never want me because I'm not pretty enough" are the inner thoughts of an anxious-preoccupied person.

"It's so hard to find a connection with other people who understand my humor and my personality" and "What's the point in a relationship? I'm just going to get hurt anyway" are the core beliefs of a dismissive-avoidant person.

On the other hand, fearful-avoidant people may have core beliefs like, "I want to do this, but I know I'll just fail" and, "If I show who I really am, people might judge me for it." Fearful-avoidant people know deep down that they deserve better. At the same time, they also find it hard to accept that reality.

The core beliefs of a secure person revolve around statements like, "I am worthy," "The world isn't out to destroy me," and "I can do this." Of course, everyone has bad days where we probably feel a bit more off than usual. For secure people, these are merely fleeting thoughts and aren't their reality.

Do you now see how damaging these beliefs are and how they affect your relationships and perspective in life? Luckily, this isn't the end of the road for all of us. There's still a way for us to transform these negative thoughts into positive ones. Simply adding "yet" to the statement, "I can't do it," completely changes things for us, don't you think?

OVERCOMING YOUR LIMITING BELIEFS

I know it seems hard trying to overcome your limiting beliefs. After all, this is what you perceived to be your reality for many years. However, there is hope. It may take time, and you will slip up occasionally, but as long as you're actively trying to better yourself every single day, you'll be fine.

To overcome your limiting beliefs, you first need to identify what they are. You must be willing to get to know yourself on a much deeper level. Think of ideas, situations, or people. Now, write down your thoughts about them. Remember a time when you had a job opportunity you wanted to take but didn't? Why didn't you? What was your thought process behind it? How did you come to that conclusion? Or go back to a time when you met someone. Everything seemed to be going great for both of you, but you didn't want to take it one step further. How come? What prompted you to reject the person? Is it because of your beliefs about relationships? Once you've identified your limiting beliefs, it's time to move on to the next step: questioning them. You could ask yourself questions like:

- How have these beliefs hindered me?
- Are these beliefs justified?
- Who or what caused me to have these beliefs?
- How long have I had these beliefs?
- What was I like before I had these beliefs?

When you start asking yourself these questions, by and by, the beliefs become weaker and irrational. Once you've taken them apart, you can proceed to the next step: overcoming them.

By now, maybe your beliefs are starting to lose all of the power they had on you. You realize that they were false realities all along that stopped you from doing the things you love and dating the people you like. Therefore, I propose five steps that can help you overcome your limiting beliefs.

1. **Examine the consequences.** Think long and hard about what would happen if you didn't get rid of these beliefs. In what way will holding on to them affect your life? Think about the consequences you will face if you don't let go of these beliefs. Don't just think about the short-term effects; think about the long-term ones, too. The more you realize the gravity of the situation, the more willing you are to make a change.

2. **Challenge your beliefs.** Whenever these doubts start to creep up on you, don't be afraid to challenge them. If you've got a tiny voice in your head telling you to stop because you can't do it, ask yourself, "But what if I can?". An even better question is, "What's the worst thing that can happen?" Challenging yourself will slowly allow you to explore the possibility of going outside of your comfort zone. It will be a complicated process, and your mind will probably try to convince you to think more negatively but trust that you can do it. If you find it too difficult to do alone, try asking for the help of a close friend or significant other. Having another rational person in the room is also a good backup.

3. **Find role models.** One way to change your beliefs is to

look for role models who defied the odds. Depending on what hobby you wanted to try but were too afraid of, do some research on people who inspire you. Your brain will try to convince you not to do it, but having proof that someone also did it can help you believe things are more attainable. By presenting evidence, it's easier to convince yourself to go out and give something a go.

4. **Affirm yourself out loud.** It may seem like a crazy idea, but it doesn't hurt to talk to yourself at times. When I'm in stressful situations, if I speak my frustrations out loud, I feel much better by the time I finish. The same goes for your affirmations. Reciting your affirmations out loud helps your brain rewire into creating healthier perceptions of yourself. Plus, hearing affirmations said out loud is a good boost for our self-esteem. If you feel too awkward at first, try mentally reciting them. Once you feel like you're ready, speak them into existence. Repeating them in front of the mirror every morning is a powerful way to start your day, too. You could start your day by saying something like, *"I am worthy. I am full of love. I deserve to be loved. I will be successful."* Remember, you attract the kind of energy you give out. You also attract the person you are. For example, if you want to attract someone fit, driven, and financially stable, you first need to be these things.

5. **Create new beliefs.** Now this one is certainly more difficult and requires more effort, but it will be worth it. I promise. This goes hand-in-hand with number four. Once you've shifted into a more confident self, it's time to go out

with the old and in with the new. Create new beliefs! Here are some new views you can acknowledge instead:

- *"It's okay if they don't like me. I like who I am. It's not my job to appease people."*
- *"I got rejected because I'm meant for better things."*
- *"I love freely because love is not a limited resource."*
- *"People deserve to be given the benefit of the doubt."*
- *"I can achieve whatever I set my heart to."*
- *"It's okay if I don't (milestone) by (age). People go through life at different paces."*

Now that you've followed all the steps, have faith that things will fall into place. However, change doesn't happen overnight, so you might go back to your limiting beliefs now and then. One way to ensure you never forget them is to write them down and maybe stick them somewhere you can always see, like on your fridge or bedroom door. Over time, your mind will start getting used to this new way of thinking and, soon enough, it will become a good habit. Don't worry. You don't have to go big right away. You can always start small by addressing some of the simpler limiting beliefs. Give yourself time to adjust to these new changes.

REPROGRAMMING YOUR ATTACHMENT STYLE

There is an interesting debate among attachment theorists about whether our attachment styles are stable and, if not, what factors contribute to this instability? Also, how long does it take for our attachment style to change? Sadly, only a few researchers have explored the different factors that may accompany the change in our attachment style. Gillath et al. (2016) found that although there was a change in a person's attachment style, these changes did not stick over time. They discovered that these changes were dependent on certain major life experiences, such as loss. However, parental relationships proved to be more stable compared to romantic relationships. Lastly, an adult's attachment style was easier to predict than a child's attachment. This further strengthens the idea that adult attachment styles are relatively stable.

However, Cozzerelli et al. (2003) presented interesting information that somewhat contradicts attachment pattern stability. They found that even though attachment patterns presented a high degree of stability, they were still susceptible to changes due to certain factors. Some of these factors are a history of abuse, psychological problems, altering life events, and other relational experiences. They also found that changes in mental health coincided with the change in attachment style. What is interesting to note, though, is that attachment styles fluctuate over time. They believe that we can shift our attachment style to adapt to current circumstances. This is what they called our "working" attachment style. But ultimately, we have a "baseline" attachment style that reflects our general views of the self and others. We are most likely to return to our "baseline" attachment style without circumstances like stress and relationship problems. However, they did believe that repeated contact with an individual can reprogram a person's inner working models and may cause a change in the baseline attachment style.

For real change to occur, our subconscious mind must first be addressed. Because it is responsible for most of our inner thoughts, we must be actively aware of stopping it. Otherwise, there can be a constant push-pull battle. We have to be willing to make a change, but having a secure partner can help us transition into a more secure attachment, too. As Cozzerelli said, repeated contact with a secure individual can cause a change in our attachment patterns. When paired with a secure partner, repetition of patterns and emotional reinforcement occurs, which can cause the individual to develop a secure attachment. But that does not mean you can't transition into a more secure attachment on your own, too.

With that said, here are five steps you can use which can help you reprogram your attachment style:

1. **Notice the patterns that trigger you.** Sometimes, when people get triggered, they go into a trance state. What happens is the body goes on autopilot, doing whatever it is supposed to be doing, while the brain ruminates on the what-ifs. For example, you could be brushing your teeth and then remember the fight you had with your partner earlier that day. Your body is still executing the action, but your subconscious has taken control of your thoughts by reinforcing your limiting beliefs on you. If you can identify the triggers, it will be easier for you to recognize it when it happens. Then, you can snap out of your trance the next time it happens. The better you are at snapping out of your trance, the more conscious control you have over your thoughts.

2. **Identify your core beliefs.** Whenever you feel triggered and damaging thoughts appear, try to identify the cause behind these thoughts. Identifying the cause behind your core beliefs will help you break them. Let's take an example from an anxious-preoccupied perspective. Suppose you are arguing with your partner. Suddenly, you begin to have thoughts about your partner leaving you. Assess why you have these thoughts. What previous experience caused you to develop this belief?

3. **Reevaluate your core beliefs.** It will be hard to reframe your core beliefs only because you believed them for so long. However, this doesn't mean it has to be your reality for the rest of your life. There will be a lot of conflicts between your conscious and subconscious minds during this time. You don't have to do a complete 180 with your thoughts if they make you uncomfortable, though. What you can do instead is reframe your perspective. Don't torture yourself by believing in these bad ideas. Your core beliefs will become more ingrained in your mind if you are incapable of snapping out of a trance.

4. **Create a new emotional response.** In times of tension, try to invest in a more positive emotional response. Stop investing in negative responses. Instead of questioning your partner's love for you in the middle of an argument, try to reassure yourself instead. Try not to worry about the future too much because it hasn't even happened yet. Instead of thinking, "Does this person even love me?" try thinking, "This person probably loves me, and this is just another

conflict we can get through. Even if they don't love me anymore, that's okay. Other people love me. I am going to be okay." Conflict is unavoidable, but you can avoid going into a trance by simply producing a new response.

5. **Take action.** The last step is to take action. By thinking, "How can I resolve this conflict?" you are simply letting your conscious mind take over and snapping out of your trance. Thus, you give your mind the power to address conflicts instead of just allowing your damaging beliefs to control the situation.

Reprogramming your attachment style will be a difficult journey and, if you are unsure whether or not you can do it alone, seeking the aid of a therapist may help. What you have to remember, though, is that you must be willing to make a change. A therapist will only be there to ask you the questions you're too afraid to ask yourself. Even if the therapist can help you unlock all of your fears and trauma, therapy will be ineffective if you are unwilling to change. I'm not saying this to discredit therapists, though. They are great and can help you truly understand why you are the way you are. But like I said, they're only there to guide you and offer insight.

As you begin to transcend your limiting beliefs, your attachment style will slowly follow suit. Soon enough, you will find yourself turning your weaknesses into your strengths. If you're willing to put in the work and rise above your circumstances, you'll wake up a more confident and secure person.

5

KNOW YOUR STRENGTHS AND WEAKNESSES

I t's time for us to talk about your strengths and weaknesses. Although the goal is for us to develop a secure attachment, that doesn't mean we're not going to celebrate the strengths of the insecurely attached. Just because you have an insecure attachment does not mean you don't carry any strengths with you. Every human on this planet has their strengths and weaknesses. Even your attachment style comes with strengths and weaknesses. Being aware of your attachment style's pros and cons can help empower you and lead you towards a more positive outlook.

The point is, we must be willing to embrace our truth. We have to accept that this is where we stand right now, flawed and insecure. From there, we must take action, but we must not forget to take patience with us. Transitioning into a more secure attachment will take time, and that's okay. Remember, Rome wasn't built in a day, so don't pressure yourself to change overnight. Life is a constant learning experience. There will be a lot of trial and error. With these errors come lessons. With lessons comes growth.

More importantly, what you must not forget is that you are strong. Despite all you've experienced, you are here, and you are learning. Your willingness alone to learn shows strength and character. For that, I'm proud of you.

THE DISMISSIVE-AVOIDANT'S STRENGTHS AND WEAKNESSES

No matter what people say about the dismissive-avoidant, they have many strengths that prove they are good people. Dismissive-avoidant people make good long-lasting friendships. These people show up effectively and are capable of connecting with their friends. They are some of the most grounded people. Furthermore, they value stability and security in their friendships.

Career-wise, dismissive-avoidant people excel in that category, too, as they have a very strong work ethic. Unfortunately, they do carry the belief that the best way to get the job done is to do it themselves. However, that is because they are detail-oriented and excel in their work. Sadly, this strong work ethic may sometimes drive them into becoming a workaholic. They may also struggle with delegating tasks which can lead to burnout. Another weakness is that they base their self-worth on the success and acknowledgment that they receive.

As for their career choices, they might be more drawn to high-risk or thrilling jobs because they get an adrenaline rush from the thrill. This is the healthiest and most acceptable release of their emotions for them. They might also enjoy a high-profile career. In contrast, this desire to perform well may overwhelm and paralyze them, so they might appear lazy and incompetent. Furthermore, this pressure they put on themselves to attain success might even lead them to shy away due to a fear of failure.

Dismissive-avoidant people are also great at analytical problem-solving. Whatever they do, they do it methodically and analytically. They are intelligent people and can be relied upon. This is because they spend a lot of time in their head whenever they don't feel safe. Although, sometimes, they spend too much time in their head trying to find a rational way out of a problem instead of trying to let their emotions lead for once. They are proud of their ability to think quickly without letting their emotions take control. In turn, this allows them to work well in crisis situations. Another strength of the dismissive-avoidant style is that they seem like they don't take things personally, making them seem like good listeners. On the other hand, this calmness might make them seem like they don't care about what's happening around them.

As distant as they seem, they believe in the greater good and root for the underdog. They especially have a soft spot for animals and people. This trait makes them irresistible to anxious-preoccupied people who admire the dismissive-avoidant's strength, self-sufficiency, and charisma. Having a soft spot for disadvantaged groups may even motivate them enough to be the voice of the underdog. This situation works with their dismissive attitude because, in a way, they are still keeping people at a distance. They are fighting for a group and not a person, so it creates an invisible barrier between them and the people they're fighting for.

Overall, dismissive-avoidant people can display healthy patterns as long as they have things that offer stability.

THE ANXIOUS-PREOCCUPIED'S STRENGTHS AND WEAKNESSES

As anxious as they seem, anxious-preoccupied people are some of the most charming and charismatic people. They possess some of the most powerful qualities you could look for in a friend. They make great friends because they show up consistently and want to be there for people. They are always looking for ways to connect and have great social skills. This means that they make friends easily.

Anxious people may be one of the most likable people out there. They are very open-hearted, warm, and loving. They are also very empathetic and sympathetic people. If you are anxious-preoccupied, other people may see you as loyal and compassionate, so they run to you for advice. Additionally, they are highly adaptable and perform well in emotional regulation. Emotional regulation can be defined as the ability to effectively manage and control one's feelings during a highly emotional experience.

If you're dating an anxious-preoccupied person, you won't feel anything less than a priority. They are very romantic and affectionate partners. They may even notice the smallest things about you and have the ability to make you feel seen. They are quick to forgive and are committed to working through any conflict you may have.

Anxious people are very thoughtful and considerate with the gifts they give.

Furthermore, they bring a level of fire and passion to the relationship and always come up with ways to impress you. The downside is that eventually, they may start to feel that all of this is a performance. They may start to feel a need to constantly think of ways to impress their partner just to keep their attention.

As mentioned before, anxious people are empathetic. They find it relatively easy to slip into someone else's shoes and see things from their perspective. The problem with this is that, over time, the intense amount of empathy may weaken their personal boundaries. If they empathize too deeply with their significant other, they may end up discrediting their own emotions. However, this is less a problem of empathy and more of a form of enmeshment. The anxious-preoccupied sees any form of conflict as an abandonment. As a result, they may lose some of their individuality.

Generosity is another trait, although this is more of a double-edged sword. Anxious-preoccupied people are very giving. They may even end up giving more than what's necessary. As a result, they tend to keep track of things in the relationship. Subconsciously, they give to get. If they find that their partner doesn't reciprocate the same amount of generosity they displayed, they hold it against themselves. They equate the amount of sacrifice they make to their self-worth.

Lastly, creativity is probably one of the most important strengths an anxious-preoccupied displays. They may spend hours dreaming up scenarios and conversations with their partners, but this is good! This means they have an immense capacity to visualize and manifest these visions. If they grew up not having any healthy models that set an example, it's their job to imagine and manifest healthy relationship models. Their capacity to visualize offers them a blueprint of what a healthy and secure relationship is supposed to look like.

THE FEARFUL-AVOIDANT'S STRENGTHS AND WEAKNESSES

People may criticize the fearful-avoidant for being hot and cold, but they also bring some really good traits to the table. For one, fearful-avoidant individuals are deeply passionate and expressive. They have a huge depth of emotion and passion that they find difficult to keep in. As a result, they may be some of the most creative people out there. They tend to really understand poetry and feel the music. There are also times when they can get lost in a painting, book, or movie. They may also be drawn to other art forms like acting and dancing.

What's more, they like digging into things and looking at them on a deeper level, so they may get things that sometimes fly over everyone else's head. They can even lose themselves in sex if they want to. The downside to this trait is that these huge waves of emotion may be so big and overwhelming that it can lead to numbness within them. That's where the hot and cold comes in; they may either show a deep passion (hot) or a complete numbness (cold).

The strengths of a fearful-avoidant are a mix of both the anxious-preoccupied and the dismissive-avoidant. Like the dismissive-avoidant, a fearful-avoidant is grounded. They don't like hanging out with friends on a superficial level. But, like the anxious-preoccupied, they can be empathetic, caring, and open-hearted.

As for the analytical side of things, fearful-avoidants are like the dismissive-avoidants because they also pay great attention to details. Furthermore, they are very determined and achievement-oriented. Their appreciation for research and novelty makes them great entrepreneurs. They work well under pressure, too.

Fearful-avoidant people tend to be highly charismatic. This is partly because they spent most of their life being hypervigilant. Now, as adults, they are extremely perceptive and are great at reading a room. However, there is a slight paradox to this skill. They are great at reading human behavior and emotions, but somehow, they find it hard to understand their own. The other downside is that they may use this charisma to attract people. Eventually, they begin to question people's intentions or affection towards them. They may start doubting whether the affection they receive is truly genuine or if it is due to their charisma. On the other hand, they may use this charisma to manipulate the people around them.

Lastly, fearful-avoidants have deep compassion for children, plants, and animals. Most of them feel truly at home when surrounded by nature and by animals. This deep compassion they possess can be manifested in how they relate to nature versus other people. The only downside to this trait is that they sometimes tend to project the negative parts of themselves onto more helpless beings. This has something to do with their past. Adults develop a fearful-avoidant attachment due to unresolved trauma from their parents. Their parents projected their trauma onto their children, and in turn, these adults may do the same thing. If this pattern isn't broken, it may result in intergenerational abuse.

THE SECURE'S STRENGTHS AND WEAKNESSES

People may tend to romanticize them, but even securely attached individuals have their pros and cons. Let's first start with their strengths. Secure people tend to be stable in relationships. They always assume their partner is well-intentioned and take their best interests into account. They are comfortable with vulnerability and feel safe being open with their partner. They are direct individuals, so if they ask for space, they will tell you exactly what they need at that moment. During an argument with their partner, there is a chance that they will raise their voice. However, they will only stick to the argument and never attack any part of your personality. They will probably be the first ones to initiate contact and conflict resolution, too. Aside from that, they are better at empathizing than sympathizing, which is most likely why they have longer-lasting relationships.

With the strengths come the weaknesses. When paired with an insecure partner, they may feel confused at the different signals their partner displays. In turn, they may feel responsible for making sure their partner is happy and satisfied. Furthermore, they tend to be clueless about their partner's coping mechanisms, so they may unknowingly trigger them without recognizing how or why. What's more, they tend to view the world from a rather naïve perspective, so they sometimes fail to establish clear boundaries. Unfortunately, they tend to compromise too much, which results in them being taken advantage of. Lastly, whenever their partner says something or acts a certain way, they take it too personally. What they don't realize is that their partner is only displaying a trauma response.

Want a summary of the strengths & weaknesses of each attachment style?
Download my attachment style "cheat sheet" by going to
MasterYourAttachmentStyle.com/CheatSheet

HOW CODEPENDENCY SHOWS UP IN YOUR ATTACHMENT STYLE

The term *codependency is* used to mean something else. Today, it is defined as "an excessive emotional, social, or sometimes physical dependence on another person."

Like most things, codependency is rooted in our childhood. There are many reasons why a person may grow up being codependent. It could be due to family dysfunction, emotional neglect, abuse (physical, emotional, verbal), or mental illness. Codependency may also be a result of a primary caregiver denying that their behavior was harmful. The primary caregiver may have also belittled or invalidated the child's emotions simply because they believed all the primary needs were met.

There are a few signs that tell if you may be codependent. Here are some of these signs:

- Ignore your own needs
- Have low self-esteem
- Feel responsible for others' emotions
- Mask pain with humor
- Fail to establish clear boundaries
- Find it hard to say no
- Feel it's your job to rescue people
- Feel valuable when others need you
- Are manipulative
- Deny your problems
- Lie to protect others and their behavior

Codependency may even be a trigger for our attachment trauma. Although it is often related to the anxious-preoccupied, it is one weakness that all insecure attachments share. However, it manifests itself in different ways. In a dismissive-avoidant attachment, the person keeps their distance to mask their true feelings and avoid rejection. For example, this may mean working extremely long hours to create some distance between them and others. For the anxious-preoccupied, codependency may be characterized as feeling insecure in relationships and fearing being alone. For example, they may assume the worst in any given situation, fearing that their partner has grown sick of them and wishes to leave. Lastly, codependency in a fearful-avoidant means craving closeness but distancing themselves when things become more intimate. An example of this is when they push people away or constantly test their loyalty. It can also be seen when they justify leaving the relationship by being critical of their partners.

Codependency isn't entirely a bad thing. Sometimes it can actually be good. Having a willingness to be vulnerable in a relationship can lead to a solid foundation. However, it becomes an issue when the person starts sacrificing their own needs for the other person. It can also feel suffocating when the person constantly seeks approval from their partner as it stops them from navigating their own life.

What one must never forget is that codependency is not your fault. It is also not a mental illness. But most importantly, it doesn't have to be forever. You are capable of unlearning these unhealthy patterns. Your relationship with yourself is the most important in your life. Therefore, healing yourself can be one of the most self-fulfilling experiences. When you catch yourself engaging in codependent behavior, ask yourself why that happens. It may have had something to do with your childhood and how love was given in your household. Was love freely given, or was it something you had to work hard to receive? When you needed support from your primary caregiver, did they show up or leave you hanging? How has this affected your view on people and love?

Once you begin to explore these questions and approach them head-on, you can begin to rewire yourself so that your relationships with people are healthy, loving, and mutually beneficial.

EMBRACING YOUR WEAKNESSES

Let's be real here: It's often hard to embrace our flaws, especially if people like pointing them out every now and then. We know nobody was born perfect, and yet we find it hard to accept our weaknesses. I think it's because we all like to believe we're superior beings. Acknowledging our flaws would mean acknowledging our failures, and that's probably something we have trouble admitting. However, I'm here to tell you that embracing your weaknesses is actually good for you. Of course, not all weaknesses are meant to be changed. No matter how much you try to improve a weakness, you will reach your maximum potential, and it's okay when that happens. Instead of trying to perfect every single flaw, how about accepting and embracing them instead? Here are a few reasons why you should embrace your flaws:

1. **It leads to self-awareness.** Having a sense of self-awareness is the most powerful tool you can carry with you. Furthermore, being aware of who you are will help you figure out things you should do to better yourself. Knowing your strengths and weaknesses allows productivity to happen. Knowing what you're good at can help you focus on them and use them to your advantage. Being aware of what you're not good at will give you the chance to work on them and improve yourself. People who pretend to be good at something are only slowing themselves down. It does more harm than good.

2. **It allows growth.** Some weaknesses seem impossible to

fix, but there are certainly those which you can improve upon. Of course, everybody has weaknesses. The more you work on your perceived shortcomings, the less of a weakness they become. One should never allow weaknesses to have control over their lives and the decisions they make. By acknowledging your weaknesses, you cannot let them hold you back from doing better. Of course, we can always do it independently, but when people get external love and support, they grow and improve more.

3. **You can establish more meaningful connections**. People appreciate others who are authentic and open. By being open about your weaknesses, you are allowing yourself to feel vulnerable in front of others. This will lead to deeper and stronger relationships with the people in your life. Once others see how authentic you are, they will also begin to allow themselves to be vulnerable around you. This is because they feel comforted by the fact that you are willing to show your deepest and most vulnerable parts to them. There is just something so raw and beautiful in being willing to show flawed parts of yourself to the people you trust.

4. **You'll be introduced to more opportunities**. When you're ready to embrace all of your weaknesses and work on them, many opportunities will be waiting for you. Working on the weaknesses you have can bring about positive changes. For example, you may have trouble setting boundaries which can often lead to you being taken advantage of. By acknowledging that you reserve the right to set boundaries, it's a step towards self-care. Only then will

you realize how many opportunities you gave up because you prioritized others' needs first before your own.

BEING IN THE MOMENT

There is power in embracing who you are. Now that we've talked about how limiting beliefs affect your life, I hope you have a clearer understanding of how your past dictates so much of your present, no matter how many years have gone by. Even though decades have passed, the mind often finds it hard to forget.

If there is one thing I want you to take away from this whole book, it's that before you begin to make changes in your life, you must first embrace who you are now. Of course, you can definitely work on yourself. Yes, you can rewire your brain into creating new and positive core beliefs. Yes, identify your strengths and weaknesses and use them to your advantage. What you should never do, though, is beat yourself up for being insecurely attached. We can do nothing to change the past, and ruminating over it prevents us from moving forward. Instead, learn to accept who you are, no matter how flawed you think you are. The key to happiness in the present is to allow yourself to be exactly who you're supposed to be.

Once you begin accepting yourself as you are, you're one step closer to a more secure attachment. As you start to navigate your relationships successfully, there is one thing you must realize. Even if you transitioned into a more secure attachment, your next relationship won't be perfect like in the movies. There is no perfect partner, and there is no perfect relationship. Therefore, don't expect your next partner to act like a fairytale character.

As you go through life, never forget to be patient with the people around you and especially with yourself. You are a work-in-progress, so it's only natural that you will make mistakes. Be kind. Be gentle. Love who you are. Ultimately, after overcoming all your limiting beliefs and working to do better, you might one day wake up to realize that you've completely shifted into a secure attachment. Who knows? You might even find yourself in a secure, healthy, lasting, and loving relationship.

SUCCESSFULLY NAVIGATING YOUR RELATIONSHIPS AND FEELING A SENSE OF SECURITY

We have now come a long way from the first chapter. So far, we've discussed why you are the way you are, the factors that may have influenced it, what your attachment style is, and your strengths and weaknesses. Now, it's time for you to learn how to navigate your relationships successfully and how to feel secure within yourself.

First things first, don't try to be something you are not. Perfect partners and perfect relationships don't exist. As you may have read in chapter 5, even the secure attachment has its flaws. The key to success in a relationship is the willingness to work on building it. A lot of people believe love is a feeling, but I believe love is a choice. When you wake up every day and try to do better than you did yesterday, that's how you know you love someone. It's completely fine if you haven't shifted into a secure attachment yet; no one will judge you for it. Don't forget, even insecure attachment styles have their strengths.

"THE ONE"

A common mistake that people make is entering into a relationship with the idea of "The One." That is a very damaging idea to have and only hinders you from seeing the bigger picture. Out of the 7.8 *billion* people in the world, do you truly believe there's only *one* person out there for you?

It's true that some people just aren't compatible together, but it's not true that there's only one person meant to be with you. Building a lasting relationship requires lots of time, effort, and commitment. Of course, the first few months, the honeymoon phase, is probably the easiest because that's when everything is new. However, when the honeymoon phase starts to fade, that's usually when the problems kick in. Suddenly, you start noticing all of their flaws. The quirks you used to find cute now annoy you to death. The things you used to find laughable are now the source of your frustrations. This is when things start to get harder, and you have to put in more work. The rose-colored glasses have been removed, and so you start questioning the value of the relationship, whether they really are "The One" for you.

See, when we believe in this idea of a soulmate, we may end up romanticizing the person or even putting them on a pedestal, and that never turns out well. Believing that you are made for this person as they are for you may cause you to stay in toxic relationships. When you romanticize a person, you begin to dismiss all of their red flags and stay simply because you believe there's no one else out there for you. Soulmates aren't real, but if they are, it's because the relationship was something they chose to build together. Relationships take a lot of trust and openness, but even that doesn't happen overnight, especially if the person has been through some toxic relationships.

I've had my fair share of frustration in relationships, so I know the feeling. However, as I grew older, I began to understand that not everyone is willing to open up one month into the relationship. Sometimes, people aren't ready to divulge their darkest secrets yet, and that's okay. It wouldn't be fair for your partner to open up to you simply because you pressured them into doing so. You should always give each other time and space to get comfortable in the relationship before digging into all the deep stuff. For people who have unresolved trauma, opening up may be a difficult task.

Ultimately, this idea of "The One" blinds us from our capacity to care for and love other people. If we get too caught up in this idea of a soulmate, we might just let the right person slip by. Furthermore, believing in this idea that the perfect person will just swoop in and fit into your heart like a missing puzzle piece will set unrealistically high expectations in relationships. The sooner we start accepting that no relationship is perfect, the easier it will be for us to be more open to the world.

NEVER ASSUME UNLESS OTHERWISE STATED

It's not a secret that humans are the most complex beings. No two people's choices are ever guided by the same thing. People might have the same end goal, but the psychological factors and experiences that lead to that goal are entirely different. Therefore, one should never assume how another person feels.

By now, you've probably heard this over and over again, but communication truly is key. Assumptions will honestly lead to nothing. The best way to address issues with your partner is to communicate with them. No matter how long you've been with your partner, never assume you know what they think and feel at that moment. Assumptions are often damaging to relationships, especially if all the person does is assume and never asks. Believing you know your partner better than they know themselves makes it seem like you're taking away their sense of agency.

The thing is, when we assume what the other is feeling, that's usually an echo of our own thoughts and emotions. This is damaging because this is not a reflection of the truth. Most, if not all, of our assumptions are based on our own feelings, hindering us from seeing the situation more objectively. Furthermore, people change and grow all the time, so you might even be holding onto an outdated assumption about them.

Lastly, assumptions stop us from truly listening to our partners. When we stop listening, we stop sharing our thoughts and vice versa. When thoughts aren't shared, conflicts are harder to resolve. When conflicts aren't resolved, couples begin to distance themselves from each other. When the distance between a couple is created, the level of intimacy in a relationship is decreased. Do you see how an innocent assumption can snowball into something much bigger and damaging to the relationship?

If you notice yourself falling into this kind of behavior, you must learn to recognize it to prevent it from happening in the future. Instead, try to focus on your partner's more positive traits. Furthermore, never forget to communicate with your partner. Instead of assuming, approach them and have a conversation. Remember to approach them openly. Being defensive does nothing to alleviate any argument and will only make it worse. When healthy communication does not exist in a relationship, true feelings are bottled up and never openly expressed. As a result, couples may have a hard time moving forward together.

LOVE YOURSELF BEFORE YOU LOVE OTHERS

These days it's rare to find a romantic movie where the protagonist does not end up with someone and chooses to go their own way. Movies and books have bombarded us with the idea that we can only know we've made it in life if we get a storybook ending. This storybook ending refers to getting married to someone. Even young kids have this idea embedded into their minds. Out of the 12 official Disney princesses, only Merida and Moana don't end up with someone by the end of the movie. Now, there is nothing wrong with believing that marriage is a storybook ending. What's wrong is believing this is the *only* way for someone to have a storybook ending.

Relationships can be great and can be one source of your happiness, but we must learn to value ourselves first before truly committing ourselves to someone. It's probably a hard pill to swallow, but you can't really love someone until you first learn how to love yourself. Likewise, you won't realize how worthy you are of love until you've loved yourself. Think of it: You love yourself 20%. Then, someone comes along and loves you 25%. You're going to think, "Wow, that's so much love!" when in reality, it's not even half what you deserve. And this is all because you never learned to love yourself 100%.

However, what people fail to realize is that we don't always need a partner to fulfill some of life's desires. One can learn to be content with their own company and appreciate the relationship one has with themselves. The best way to truly get to know yourself is to do things alone. People might think it's sad and lonely for you to be going out to the movies alone, but how else are you supposed to get to know yourself better? When people constantly surround you, most of the decisions you make will be based on what is most convenient for everyone involved. However, when you're alone, that's when you're free to make any decision you want without ever feeling guilty about it.

By focusing on self-love, you give yourself time to heal from your wounds, whether from past relationships or your childhood. The healing process is filled with ups and downs, but it can be one of the most rewarding things ever when paired with self-love. It is only through self-love that we learn how worthy we are of so many things in life. Saying no becomes easier because we know our time is valuable, and we don't want it wasted on people who won't appreciate our presence.

However, the best thing about learning to love yourself is growing comfortable in your own skin. When you finally realize how worthy you are, you stop seeking approval from the people around you. You begin to realize that no amount of external approval will ever satisfy you because confidence needs to come from within you. In return, you start caring less about public opinion and start doing things you genuinely like. Furthermore, you become more accepting when you mess up. You understand that you won't wake up every day ready to face the world, and so you are more ready to forgive yourself for having bad days. And even when you wake up on the wrong side of the bed, you are still your own cheerleader.

Did you know that reading this book is an act of self-love, too? The fact that you picked up this book with the intent of getting to know more about your attachment style and how to shift into a secure attachment is proof that you're working on yourself. If you never cared about your happiness, you probably wouldn't have bothered learning about attachment theory or your past traumas in the first place.

There's no shortcut to loving yourself, just like there's no standard process to achieving self-love. Like most things, loving yourself requires time and conscious effort. But when you finally reach the point where you know you've got your own back through thick and thin, it can be the most satisfying feeling.

MEETING YOUR OWN NEEDS

In chapter 2, we discussed Anthony Robbins' concept of the six basic human needs. Our needs are an extensive part of who we are. These needs are ranked based on what we perceive we lacked the most. For example, if you value family, emotional connection, and security above all else, you'd consider yourself family-oriented. This could be because, as a child, you had a dysfunctional family, and that is something you don't want to experience in your relationships.

However, a problem arises when we fail to identify what our needs are on a deeper level. A lack of awareness of our needs means we disempower ourselves and minimize our ability to feel fulfilled. This may lead to a lack of direction or a lack of purpose in life.

To identify what your needs are, you must look within. Think to yourself, "Okay, what is it that I need?" If you believe you need affection the most, think about what you feel when this need is met. Do you feel safe and comforted when your partner is affectionate? Then, think about what human need that translates to. In this scenario, this meets the need for certainty.

But before we can have our needs met by others, we must first have a detailed understanding of our six basic human needs and develop strategies to get those needs met. Furthermore, we must first fill our own cup halfway before asking others to fill it for us. If we never know how to fill our own cup halfway, it may lead to seeking to have those needs from others out of sheer desperation. We may rely on others to fulfill our needs because we can't do it independently.

On the other hand, if we learn to fill our cup halfway, we don't put up with things that do nothing to serve us. Additionally, when we meet someone who does help fulfill those needs, we can approach it from a space of healthy non-attachment instead of desperation. To be in a healthy relationship, we must first do the work and meet our own needs at least halfway before asking others to fill in what is missing.

WHAT A HEALTHY RELATIONSHIP LOOKS LIKE

It's important to identify what an unhealthy relationship looks like. However, it is equally as important to identify what a healthy relationship looks like. People are often unsure of what they want in a relationship. If they grew up in a toxic environment, they don't have a model for what a healthy relationship should look like, so sometimes they end up asking for crumbs even though they deserve much more than that.

With that being said, some traits define what a healthy relationship should look like. Here are 10 of those traits:

1. **Trust.** This is probably the most important trait. Hence, it's at the top of the list. If trust doesn't exist between two people in a relationship, there is no solid foundation they can lean on. Without trust, it would be difficult to create emotional intimacy as both people always question the other's intentions and doubt their capability to stay faithful in the relationship. People who have constantly been subjected to hurtful experiences might develop trust issues, and they have every right to. However, it would be unfair to crucify someone for a sin they haven't even committed. Trust takes time to build, which is understandable. But one shouldn't refuse to trust their partner because of someone else's mistakes.

2. **Pacing.** A new relationship can be one of the most exhilarating experiences of your life. However, it is

important to remember that it should be kept at a pace that feels comfortable for both of you. Don't jump into major milestones together if both of you aren't completely ready for them. Of course, chances are you spend lots of time together, but you must both agree with the rate at which you are moving. In a healthy relationship, the pace feels right; you don't feel pressured in any way that causes you to take huge leaps and make you feel overwhelmed.

3. **Kindness.** You might be familiar with the saying that goes, "You can tell a lot about someone's personality based on how they treat service workers." Service workers are people like us, and if your partner sees them as "inferior" just because they earn a lower wage, then maybe you should run in the other direction. Beauty and riches are superficial; you can always find those traits in someone. What is rare, though, is kindness. If you choose a partner, choose someone kind. A simple act of kindness goes a long way. Also, kindness is such an important thing because you never know what people are going through in their personal life. You never know how many lives you'll touch by simply choosing to be kind.

4. **Communication.** This is one trait that's worth repeating over and over again. Communicating openly is something that doesn't come naturally for some people. It could be because they were conditioned to bury their feelings for the sake of keeping the peace or for keeping up appearances. Or it could be because, as children, we never learned to acknowledge our own emotions. Nonetheless,

communication is a vital trait in a healthy relationship. It would be difficult for you to get through conflicts if you constantly suppress your emotions and don't communicate with your partner. This goes back to what was said about assuming your partner's feelings.

5. **Respect.** Just because you are romantically involved with someone doesn't mean you have to have the same beliefs and opinions. Remember, you are your own person, just as they are their own person, so it would be unhealthy for you to impose all your beliefs onto them and vice versa. Furthermore, you should be respectful of each other's boundaries. Both of you lead different lives, so you must learn to respect that they may also want to hang out with other people and do something else. A healthy relationship that practices respect involves supporting each other's dreams and aspirations, being a cheerleader through the ups and downs, and appreciating each other.

6. **Flexibility.** You might be aware that relationships require lots of compromises, and the key to having a healthy relationship, despite the compromises, is to be flexible. In a healthy and loving relationship, both partners are willing to bend to make room for growth. They can also evaluate how a certain decision could affect them both and then decide who should make the compromise. However, if only one person does the bending all the time, it could result in a toxic relationship. And if both people aren't willing to be flexible and make a compromise, the relationship will be over before you know it.

7. **Independence.** One must never make their world revolve around their partner. You should always have space to do your own thing outside of the relationship. This could mean going out with your own set of friends, discovering new hobbies, or just spending some alone time. Your partner doesn't need to be involved in every aspect of your life, just like you shouldn't be involved in theirs. Understand that, despite being in a relationship, having a sense of autonomy is still important lest we lose our sense of self.

8. **Honesty.** Trust and honesty are like two peas in a pod. Don't break your partner's trust by lying to them. The same goes for building trust. Trust has to be earned, but it will never be given if you constantly lie to them. In a healthy relationship, you will never feel like you have to hide your feelings around your partner. The truth may sometimes hurt, but it is always better to find out from the person directly rather than from someone else. But of course, if you have something to say that you fear is too honest, lay it down gently. They may get hurt, but they will appreciate the fact that you were honest about it.

9. **Accountability.** No perfect relationship exists, so you will have occasional arguments with your partner. You may spend hours playing the blame game in a toxic relationship until eventually, both of you just give up and stop speaking to each other. Both of you will refuse to be held accountable for the words spoken and the effect they had on each partner. On the other hand, in a healthy relationship, both of you are willing to accept when you've made a mistake. You

acknowledge your faults, and your apologies are genuine. Furthermore, you continuously make amends and try to better the relationship. When people practice **accountability,** they acknowledge how their words and actions may have affected the other person, even if that was never their intention.

10. **Fun.** Lastly, a healthy relationship is fun. You enjoy being with your partner, and days spent with them are almost always fun. Of course, the occasional argument can't be avoided. No relationship is 100% fun. There will be some lows as well. However, the good times must outweigh the bad ones. Being in a healthy relationship means you bring out the best in each other. You are not afraid of letting loose, showing your goofy side, and sharing a good laugh together. It will never weigh you down. Instead, it will always be there to lift your spirits.

CREATING A HEALTHY AND CONSCIOUS RELATIONSHIP

Maybe you're currently at a crossroads with your romantic relationship. Does your partner refuse to acknowledge attachment theory? If so, would it be healthy for you to stay even though your partner refuses to be conscious about their feelings and past? Before we answer that question, we must first ask what it means to be conscious? Do you define consciousness as having the free will to choose how you'll react in a situation? In that case, you might be a bit misguided.

Consciousness doesn't mean that you are aware of your feelings and have complete control over them. Instead, consciousness means learning how to be in a relationship where you allow your feelings to be expressed instead of trying to push them down. When you are in a conscious relationship, you continue to love your partner regardless of what stage they are in their progress.

Even though you are aware of your attachment style and acknowledge how your past trauma has affected you, that doesn't fully mean you are in a conscious relationship. This can best be represented with the statement, "I can't grow unless my partner grows together with me. If I continue to stay in the relationship, it's unhealthy and holding me back from growth." In this case, the person equates love with need satisfaction, and those should be two separate things.

Here are five tools you can use to build a healthy and conscious relationship:

- **Learn to listen.** In this current day and age, listening is one of the most important tools we need to maintain a healthy and conscious relationship. These days, many of us only listen to prepare to defend ourselves, but not to really hear what the person is saying. When you take time to really listen to your partner, this means giving them 100% of your time and attention when they're talking to you. You'll be surprised at how much you'll learn about your partner if you take the time to truly listen to them.
- **Accept your partner for who they are.** Many couples break up after a few months because they get

disappointed when they fail to "change" their partners. This is more common with women conditioned to think it's their job to turn the bad boy into the good boy. But the reality is, we can't force others to change for us; they should be willing to make the change themselves. Instead of drowning in misery when you can't force your partner to change, why not try accepting them for who they are instead, flaws and all? You can encourage them, of course, but you can't force them if they don't want to. Remember, a conscious mind loves their partner regardless of what stage they are in their progress.

- **Work on being the right person.** Instead of obsessing over the existence of a "soulmate" and a "perfect person," why not try being the right person instead? Relationships take a lot of work. There is no perfect partner because everyone has flaws. If you search the world with the idea of a perfect person, that just might lead you to jump from one relationship to the next, thinking the next person must be "The One." There is no perfect relationship either, so save yourself from heartbreak and work on yourself instead. Working on being the right person allows you to bring out the best in yourself.

- **Learn to apologize.** This is the easiest tool you can use whenever you are in an argument with your partner. For many of us who grew up in a household where our parents never acknowledged their mistakes and apologized, an apology is one thing we most appreciate. Apologizing is sometimes hard because it means swallowing your pride. But if you love your partner, the relationship should matter more than your pride. Plus, learning to apologize leads to trust, and trust is what makes a relationship healthy. So, do apologize when you make a mistake and make sure it's genuine. There is also no time limit on an apology. Therefore, don't hesitate to offer one to your partner for something you did in the past. They will appreciate the gesture.

- **Don't be afraid to ask.** This is something that many anxious-preoccupied and fearful-avoidant individuals need to learn. Stop being a people-pleaser, and don't be afraid to ask for what you want. This goes for the dismissive-avoidants, too—don't be afraid to ask for help. So many of us are afraid to ask because we're afraid of rejection or afraid of being seen as weak. But I'm here to tell you that it doesn't matter. Your partner is there to support you and be someone you can lean on in difficult times. Furthermore, being open about your needs only deepens the relationship you have, and that's a good thing.

No one can dictate how you should feel except you. Therefore, developing a sense of security is up to you. But of course, before you can truly feel secure, you must first learn to be comfortable with yourself. Don't rush into relationships just because you need company. Spend time to get to know yourself. Only then will you know what you truly want and need in a partner and yourself.

Once you're ready to step back into the world of dating, don't forget what you learned about yourself. When you finally meet someone you want to date, allow space for the relationship to grow. Sadly, it's not always a walk in the park. You might still meet a partner you're not compatible with. But if you feel secure within yourself, you'll be alright.

CONCLUSION

At last, we've come to the end of this book. It's been quite a journey, hasn't it? As we have gone through the book, we've learned many things that have helped us finally understand why we are the way we are.

The data can be traced back to John Bowlby, Mary Ainsworth, Cindy Hazan, and Philip Shaver. These are the people we should thank for coming up with the idea of attachment theory in children and adults. If they had never been curious about the attachment in maternal and romantic relationships, we probably would never have learned that the quality of care and affection we received from our parents when we were children would make such a huge impact on who we are as adults. It affected how we viewed relationships and how we looked at the world and how we perceive ourselves.

It is important to note that physical abuse isn't the only contributing factor to trauma. Children may also have trauma due to emotional abuse, enmeshment, and other, less subtle forms of abuse. Children who were subjected to abuse then develop insecure attachment styles: anxious-preoccupied, dismissive-avoidant, and fearful-avoidant. Each attachment style has different root causes. For example, adults with a fearful-avoidant attachment are most likely victims of intergenerational abuse and their parents' unresolved trauma, which was then projected onto them.

On the other hand, dismissive-avoidant individuals may have had parents that never paid attention to their needs. An adult may have an anxious-preoccupied attachment because their parents' love when they were kids was conditional. Thus, they believed they were only worthy of love if they put others' needs before their own.

Because attachment is both a biological and social necessity, the trauma we carry directly affects our lives. It even affects our mental, psychological, and physiological development. The first few years of our life are vital because it sets the tone for who we will be. So, our parents' affection and our environment impact us more than we think.

Of course, knowing our attachment style matters. The main reason for this is so that we understand why we are the way we are now. Furthermore, it helps us identify our core wounds that led to the development of this attachment style. By recognizing our core wounds, we also understand why we rank our six basic human needs differently from other people. For example, you may rank certainty higher than contribution, whereas your partner values significance more than love and connection.

The beautiful thing about attachment theory is that we get to know ourselves on a deeper and more personal level as we go along. This includes recognizing why you fight instead of freeze when faced with conflict. Additionally, even though you may have an insecure attachment, you are still graced with some very powerful strengths. Once you start to have more control over yourself, you can use these strengths to your advantage and build meaningful relationships. Our strengths go hand in hand with our weaknesses. Although the word has a negative connotation, we can get something good out of our weaknesses. Learning to accept and embrace them leads to self-awareness and provides us with potential for growth.

But for us to move to a more secure attachment, we must first be willing to embrace the trauma that we carry. Then, we must learn to overcome our limiting beliefs so they stop controlling how we see ourselves, others, and the world. We may not be able to turn back time and prevent the trauma from happening, but we won't allow it to take control over our lives anymore with the awareness we now have. For you to overcome your flawed core beliefs, you must first examine how they affected your life. Then, be ready to challenge the thoughts as they creep up on you. Next, find role models who inspire you to defy the odds. Next, and this is probably the most important, affirm yourself out loud. And finally, create healthy, new beliefs. If we can overcome our limiting beliefs, we have now rid ourselves of the many obstacles that hindered us from doing things we wanted and dating people we liked.

From now on, you should be in charge of writing your story. You have the power to move into a place of security. Even though that takes a lot of time and conscious effort, you will get there. Healing takes lots of time, but we will never heal if we don't learn to accept who we are. But the most important thing in rewiring our attachment style into a more secure one is to practice self-love. Only when you learn to love yourself can you have the capacity to love others.

With the steps we mentioned in chapter 6, you now can successfully navigate your personal and romantic relationships. To have more control over how you react to relationships, you must first get rid of the notion that a soulmate exists. Even if a soulmate did exist, they're not found—they're made. There is no such thing as a perfect relationship. There will be a lot of ups and downs. Being with someone romantically takes a lot of commitment, effort, trust, and honesty. That is something that doesn't just magically fall into your lap. I believe anyone can be your lifelong partner as long as you're both willing to put in some work to make it last.

You should have the tools you need to move from a place of insecure attachment to secure attachment from here on. If you want to be in a healthy and loving relationship, you must actively listen to your partner. It is also important that you accept them for who they are. Of course, you can always encourage them to do better, but it is never your job to "fix" them. Instead of trying to mold them and the relationship into what you want it to be, try working on becoming the right person. Once your partner sees how much effort you put into wanting to do better, you'll surely inspire them to do the same. Another key to having a lasting relationship is learning to say sorry.

When you feel that you've wronged your partner, apologize. If they felt hurt because of something you unintentionally did or said, apologize. There is nothing embarrassing about admitting you've messed up. Lastly, never be too afraid to ask for help and ask for what you want. You are worthy, and your needs are worthy. You are not as insignificant as you make yourself out to be. Your partner will never shun you for asking. Instead, they will be there to offer help and support at all times.

Life is all about the choices that you make, the people you choose to hang around with, and the moments you choose to cherish. We only have one life. It'd be a shame if we spent the entirety of it not trying to better ourselves and our relationship with the people in our lives.

Thank you for sharing this journey with me. I hope by the time you finish this book, you have enough background knowledge and tips on how to build a loving and lasting relationship. Don't worry. I don't expect you to magically have a secure attachment when the morning comes. You will sometimes stumble and go back to your old habits. Keep going. I am proud of you for what you've accomplished already.

Please remember to leave an honest review of this book on Amazon or Audible so you can let me and others know what you think. Until next time.

REFERENCES

- -, Jodie. (2019, August 21). *What are the Most Common Limiting Beliefs?* Simple Minded. https://www.simpleminded.life/most-common-limiting-beliefs

- Alessi, H., Ahn, B., Kulkin, H., & Ballard, M. (2011). *An Exploratory Study: Lesbian Identity Development And Attachment Style.* Retrieved from http://counselingoutfitters .com/vistas/vistas11/Article_72.pdf

- Anyika, R. (2021, February 17). *Enmeshment Trauma, If Your Parents' Needs Took Priority and How This Impacts Your Relationships.* Emotion Enhancement. https://www. emotionenhancement.com/single-post/enmeshment-trauma-and-how-it-impacts-your-relationships

- Bartholomew, K. (1990). *Avoidance of Intimacy: An*

Attachment Perspective. Journal of Social and Personal Relationships, 7(2), 147–178. https://doi.org/10.1177/0265407590072001

- Bartholomew, K., & Shaver, P. R. (1998). *Methods Of Assessing Adult Attachment: Do They Converge?* In J. A. Simpson & W. S. Rholes (Eds.), Attachment theory and close relationships (p. 25–45). The Guilford Press.
- Bonior, A. (2018, December 28). *What Does a Healthy Relationship Look Like?* Psychology Today. https://www.psychologytoday.com/us/blog/friendship-20/201812/what-does-healthy-relationship-look
- Bowlby, J. (1999). *Attachment and Loss.* [New York]: Basic Books.
- Bretherton, I. (2010). *Fathers in Attachment Theory and Research: A Review.* Early Child Development and Care, 180(1-2), 9–23. https://doi.org/10.1080/03004430903414661
- Bretherton, I. (2013). *Revisiting Mary Ainsworth's Conceptualization and Assessments of Maternal Sensitivity-Insensitivity.* Attachment & Human Development, 15(5-6), 460–484. https://doi.org/10.1080/14616734.2013.835128
- Brown, J., & Trevethan, R. (2010). *Shame, Internalized Homophobia, Identity Formation, Attachment Style, and the Connection to Relationship Status in Gay Men.* American Journal of Men's Health, 4(3), 267–276. https://doi.org/10.1177/1557988309342002

- Brown, G. L., Mangelsdorf, S. C., & Neff, C. (2012). *Father Involvement, Paternal Sensitivity, and Father–Child Attachment Security in the First 3 Years.* Journal of Family Psychology, 26(3), 421–430. https://doi.org/10.1037/a0027836

- Cassidy, J., Jones, J. D., & Shaver, P. R. (2013). *Contributions Of Attachment Theory and Research: A Framework for Future Research, Translation, and Policy.* Development and Psychopathology, 25(4 Pt 2), 1415–1434. https://doi.org/10.1017/S0954579413000692

- Connors, M. E. (1997). *The Renunciation of Love: Dismissive Attachment and Its Treatment.* Psychoanalytic Psychology, 14(4), 475–493. https://doi.org/10.1037/h0079736

- Cozzarelli, C., Karafa, J. A., Collins, N. L., & Tagler, M. J. (2003). *Stability and Change In Adult Attachment Styles: Associations With Personal Vulnerabilities, Life Events, and Global Construals Of Self and Others.* Journal of Social and Clinical Psychology, 22(3), 315–346. https://doi.org/10.1521/jscp.22.3.315.22888

- Dawson NK. From Uganda to Baltimore to Alexandra Township: *How Far Can Ainsworth's Theory Stretch?.* S Afr J Psychiat. 2018;24(0), a1137. https://doi.org/10.4102/sajpsychiatry.V24i0.1137

- Dutton, D.G., Saunders, K., Starzomski, A. and Bartholomew, K. (1994), *Intimacy-Anger and Insecure Attachment as Precursors of Abuse in Intimate Relationships.* Journal of Applied Social Psychology, 24:

1367-1386. https://doi.org/10.1111/j.1559-1816.
1994.tb01554

- Erozkan, Atilgan. (2016). *The Link Between Types of Attachment and Childhood Trauma.* Universal Journal of Educational Research. 4. 1071-1079. https://doi.org/10. 13189/ujer.2016.040517

- Favez, N., & Tissot, H. (2019). *Fearful-Avoidant Attachment: A Specific Impact on Sexuality? Journal of Sex & Marital Therapy,* 45(6), 510–523. https://doi.org/ 10.1080/0092623x.2019.1566946

- Feeney, Brooke. (2007). *The Dependency Paradox in Close Relationships: Accepting Dependence Promotes Independence.* Journal of personality and social psychology. https://doi.org/10.1037/0022-3514.92.2.268

- Fox, A. (2017, March 27). *10 Tools for Building Better Relationships.* Beliefnet. https://www.beliefnet.com/ wellness/galleries/10-tools-for-building-better-relationships.aspx

- Fraley, R. C. (2018). *A Brief Overview of Adult Attachment Theory and Research.* http://labs.psychology.illinois.edu/ ~rcfraley/attachment.htm.

- George, A. (2019, March 28). *10 Reasons Why Self-Love is the Best, Most Important Type Of Love.* YourTango. https://www.yourtango.com/2019322014/reasons-why-self-love-best-type-of-love-yourself-first

- Gibson, T. (2020, December 25). *The 5 Major Strengths of Each Attachment Style.* YouTube. https:// youtu.be/AsvGJau2DMM

- Gibson, T. (2020, May 4). *5 Powerful Steps to Actually Change & Reprogram Your Attachment Style at the Subconscious Level.* YouTube. https://youtu.be/NhpJ_qkjmKI

- Gibson, T. (2020, September 23). *All Insecure Attachment Styles & Their Trauma Responses.* YouTube. https://youtu.be/KCittxyTwiY

- Gillath, Omri & Karantzas, Gery & Fraley, R.. (2016). *How Stable Are Attachment Styles in Adulthood?* ScienceDirect. https://doi.org/10.1016/B978-0-12-420020-3.00006-2

- Gillath, Omri & Karantzas, Gery & Fraley, R.. (2016). *What is the Attachment Behavioral System? And, How is it Linked to Other Behavioral Systems?* ScienceDirect. https://doi.org/10.1016/B978-0-12-420020-3.00008-6

- Gray, K. L. (2011). *Effects of Parent-Child Attachment on Social Adjustment and Friendship in Young Adulthood.* Cal Poly. https://digitalcommons.calpoly.edu/psycdsp/22

- Hazan, C., & Shaver, P. (1987). *Romantic Love Conceptualized as an Attachment Process.* Journal of Personality and Social Psychology, 52(3), 511–524. https://doi.org/10.1037/0022-3514.52.3.511

- Henderson, A.J.Z., Bartholomew, K., Trinke, S.J. et al. *When Loving Means Hurting: An Exploration of Attachment and Intimate Abuse in a Community Sample.* J Fam Viol 20, 219 (2005). https://doi.org/10.1007/s10896-005-5985-y

- Jain, N. (2015). *Father-Daughter Attachment Pattern and its Influence on Daughter's Development.*

- Kamza, A. *Attachment to Mothers and Fathers During*

Middle Childhood: An Evidence From Polish Sample. BMC Psychol 7, 79 (2019). https://doi.org/10.1186/s40359-019-0361-5

- Landolt, M. A., Bartholomew, K., Saffrey, C., Oram, D., & Perlman, D. (2004). *Gender Nonconformity, Childhood Rejection, and Adult Attachment: A Study of Gay Men.* Archives of sexual behavior, 33(2), 117–128. https://doi.org/10.1023/b:aseb.0000014326.64934.50

- Leo, B. (2017, November 5). *What Is Attachment and Why is it Important? Psych Central.* https://psychcentral.com/lib/what-is-attachment-and-why-is-it-important

- Levy, T. on A. (2017, May 26). *Four Styles Of Adult Attachment.* Evergreen Psychotherapy Center. https://www.evergreenpsychotherapycenter.com/styles-adult-attachment

- MacWilliam, B. (2019, August 19). *3 Steps to Create a Truly Conscious Relationship [Secure Attachment].* YouTube. https://youtu.be/32SdVr3fgpE

- MacWilliam, B. (2020, January 16). *3 Strengths of the Open Heart.* YouTube. https://youtu.be/Z2RjSP7p31c

- MacWilliam, B. (2020, January 23). *3 Strengths of the Spice of Lifer [Fearful Avoidance].* YouTube. https://www.youtube.com/watch?v=Bbac8ywP0UY

- MacWilliam, B. (2020, January 9). *4 Strengths of the Rolling Stone [Avoidant Attachment].* YouTube. https://youtu.be/iBG5EtQN0_o

- McCullar, J. (2020, May 21). *What You Need to Know About Enmeshment Trauma.* Janet McCullar: Child

Custody and Parental Alienation Lawyer. https://
janetmccullar.com/blog/enmeshment-trauma

- McLeod, S. A. (2017, February 05). *Attachment Theory.*
Simply Psychology. https://www.
simplypsychology.org/attachment.html

- Meurisse, T. (2015, September 24). *These 6 Amazing
Things Will Happen When You Embrace Your
Weaknesses.* Lifehack. https://www.lifehack.org/313846/
these-6-amazing-things-will-happen-when-you-embrace-
your-weaknesses

- Morin, A. (2018, September 14). *3 Types of Self-Limiting
Beliefs That Will Keep You Stuck in Life (and What to Do
About Them).* Inc.com. https://www.inc.com/amy-morin/
3-types-of-unhealthy-beliefs-that-will-drain-your-mental-
strength-make-you-less-effective.html

- N/A, N. A. (2020, October 27). *10 Signs of a Healthy
Relationship.* One Love Foundation. https://www.
joinonelove.org/signs-healthy-relationship

- Naftulin, J. (2019, January 14). *Codependency is an Often
Misunderstood Buzzword, But Being 'Needy' Can
Actually Be A Good Thing.* Insider. https://www.insider.
com/what-is-codependency-2019-1

- Ndonga, E. (2018, February 20). *Why it is Important to
Embrace Your Weaknesses.* Potentash. https://www.
potentash.com/2018/02/20/important-embrace-your-
weaknesses-lifestyle/

- Oliveira P, Fearon P. *The Biological Bases of Attachment.*
Adoption & Fostering. 2019;43(3):274-293. Sage Journals.

https://journals.sagepub.com/doi/10.
1177/0308575919867770

- Ridge, S. R., & Feeney, J. A. (1998). *Relationship History and Relationship Attitudes in Gay Males and Lesbians: Attachment Style and Gender Differences*. The Australian and New Zealand journal of psychiatry, 32(6), 848–859. https://doi.org/10.3109/00048679809073875

- Robbins, T. (2020, May 1). *6 Human Needs: Do You Need to Feel Significant?* TonyRobbins.com. https://www.tonyrobbins.com/mind-meaning/do-you-need-to-feel-significant

- Schrader, J. (2019, December 10). *Move on From Trauma and Choose to Be Happy*. Psychology Today. https://www.psychologytoday.com/us/blog/prescriptions-life/201912/move-trauma-and-choose-be-happy

- Sicinski, A. (2021, March 30). *The Complete Guide on How to Overcome Your Limiting Beliefs*. IQ Matrix Blog. https://blog.iqmatrix.com/limiting-beliefs

- Vanderpuye, J. (2019, February 22). *10 Useful Tools to Improve Your Relationship*. HavingTime. https://havingtime.com/10-useful-tools-to-improve-your-relationship

- Weisberger, M. (2016, May 2). *Why Are Human Babies So Helpless?* LiveScience. https://www.livescience.com/54605-why-are-babies-helpless.html

- Winston, R., & Chicot, R. (2016). *The Importance of Early Bonding on the Long-Term Mental Health and Resilience of Children*. London journal of primary care, 8(1), 12–14. https://doi.org/10.1080/17571472.2015.1133012

- Tjaden, Cathelijn & Mulder, Cornelis & Delespaul, Philippe & Arntz, Arnoud & Kroon, Hans. (2020). *Attachment as a Framework to Facilitate Empowerment For People With Severe Mental Illness.* Psychology and Psychotherapy Theory Research and Practice. https://doi.org/10.1111/papt.12316

Lightning Source UK Ltd.
Milton Keynes UK
UKHW011135100122
396908UK00001B/106